Needful Notes on Life

Devotions to Start Your Day

By

Nina Toth

NEEDFUL NOTES ON LIFE
Devotions to Start Your Day

Copyright © 2016 Nina Toth

Welcome!

If I am to have one purpose, it is to lead people to the cross of Jesus Christ.

My friends, this life is but a vapor. Eternal life in heaven is forever. No one likes to think about leaving this life. But the truth is, we never know when we are breathing our last breath.

I used to be petrified at the thought of death and dying. That is because I was unsure of the reality of heaven and God. But I now am 100 percent positive God is alive and Jesus is Lord!

I love you, my friends. Please take a moment to pray so that your eternal life is assured. There are no strings attached. No hidden agendas. Just say it with me:

> "Lord Jesus, I confess I am a sinner. I believe You died for my sins. Please forgive me. I ask You to come into my heart. I believe You are my Savior. I believe heaven is my home. Change my life and make it count for You. I thank You, Lord. Amen."

January 1

I have just begun this journey,
Though I traveled many roads,
I have walked through many valleys,
But, I still have far to go.
The distance that's behind me,
Can never quite compare,
With the road that's been assigned me,
There is more to meet me there.
This labor will not take me,
Nor encompass my whole being,
I will not focus on my pain,
But dwell on godly things.
I feel alone most all the time,
Though I know He's by my side,
It's when the road gets winding,
I sense He's there to guide.
I know there is an end somewhere,
A final destination,
Right now, at this point in time,
I pray for a vacation.
Who am I, what's my name?
Can you guess my vocation?
I'm Jesus Christ, the very one
Who lived all your emotions.

So, since Christ suffered in the flesh for us, for you, arm
yourselves with the same thought and purpose [patiently to
suffer rather than fail to please God].
1 Peter 4:1 (AMPCE)

January 2

Are you an orphan?

You do not have to be "parentless" to have an orphan's heart. Many people experience rejection, hurt, and heartbreak, and hold onto it for life, to their detriment. Without God to heal the emotional pain, most try in vain to mend the fragmented, painful areas of years past.

A Band-Aid does no more than to cover up a wound. It does not serve to heal. Yet people will cover up and hide hurt with entrapments, such as material pleasures. It may serve as a temporary salve. But the pain returns.

What a sad way to exist.

Our God shows us how to get rid of the emotional pain by handing it all over to the burden-bearer:

But he was pierced for our transgressions, he was crushed

for our iniquities; the punishment that brought us peace

was on him, and by his wounds we are healed.

Isaiah 53:5 (NIV)

January 3

Grace, grace, how very wonderful is the mercy and love of our heavenly Father. Who sees past our many imperfections and shortcomings. Who loves us much more than we deserve. Whose unwavering gaze never turns away nor hedge of protection ever relinquishes. His mighty grasp is steady and firm. The love that reigns forever, is deeper than the ocean, higher than the mountains, and stronger than the cross that held our Savior. It is a forever, never-to-be-broken contract. None of us is exempt, unless we exclude ourselves by rejecting His invitation.

Glorious Jesus, who paid our eternal ransom, how awesome is Your Love!

January 4

Be at a point in your life where you want the very best God has for you. Sometimes in life we settle for seconds. Could it be we think we are not deserving of the "most" simply because we feel like the "least"?

Jesus said, "As you did it to one of the least of these my brothers, you did it to me" (Matthew 25:40 ESV). That also includes what we think and speak about ourselves. Being kind to ourselves means we embrace the truth that we are "the righteousness of God" in Christ (2 Corinthians 5:21 NIV).

Let's make a conscious choice to be the way God wants us to be. We can say, "Lord, let Your will be done in my life. I want more of You and less of me."

So then [God's gift] is not a question of human will and human effort, but of God's mercy. [It depends not on one's own willingness nor on his strenuous exertion as in running a race, but on God's having mercy on him.]
Romans 9:16 (AMPCE)

January 5

In the lifelong pursuit for happiness and success, do not lose sight of the true beauty in the simple things while aiming for the stars. Sometimes our dreams are lofty, and while it is good to set standards, we may get lost in ourselves along the way. Unrealistic goals sets the bar height to perfection, a place where we will only achieve despair.

Let us learn to find joy in the journey by reaching out, instead of looking within.

Let a primary goal for the day be, "Who can I bless?"

Seeking God for guidance and loving on His kids is more rewarding than just being a recipient of one's own bliss.

The LORD is my strength and shield. I trust him with all my heart. He helps me, and my heart is filled with joy. I burst out in songs of thanksgiving.

Psalm 28:7 (NLT)

January 6

God's perfect peace (*shalom* in Hebrew) is not obtained by maintaining and controlling our outward environment, but rather is the assurance of His presence in any situation.

A prime illustration of this: A contest was once held for artists to create a picture of something that depicts peace. Thousands of artists presented work of art with babbling brooks, trees, mountains, and other tranquil scenery. But the piece that took the prize showed a ferocious storm. In the painting, lightning bolts flashed and strong winds bent the boughs of a tree. Upon one of the branches of that tree, though, sat a nest with a momma bird and her babies.

In the throes of this storm, the mother bird shielded her young in the shelter of her wings. Likewise, no matter what storm life may bring our way, we may also find shelter in the shadow of our Father's wings.

Keep me as the apple of your eye; hide me in the shadow of your wings.

Psalm 17:8 (NIV)

January 7

In casting all our cares upon God, we are taking a giant step
of faith. We are believing and holding to His promise that
He will supply our every need. We continue to walk in
building faith by holding fast to His Word. In studying
God's Word daily, we are engraving His promises upon our
heart and in our minds. By doing this, we remain
strengthened and empowered, well equipped for anything
that will come our way.

Let us pray to the Lord to help us to know without a
doubt that He is in control. He cares for our every need
because He cares for us. God's Word says that He has
engraved us on the palm of His hand and that nothing and
no one can remove us from His mighty grasp.

Behold, I have engraved you on the palms of my hands.
Isaiah 49:16 (ESV)

January 8

When I have these days so bleak,

I do not think You have forgotten me.

It is at these times, I realize,

You are with me the most.

I feel You close,

Breathing on me,

Caressing me,

Whispering in my spirit's ear,

"I am here, do not despair."

I feel the warmth right from Your palm,

Your Love and peace, how blanket-soft.

Blessed be the God and Father of our Lord Jesus Christ, the Father of sympathy (pity and mercy) and the God [Who is the Source] of every comfort (consolation and encouragement), Who comforts (consoles and encourages) us in every trouble (calamity and affliction), so that we may also be able to comfort (console and encourage) those who are in any kind of trouble or distress, with the comfort (consolation and encouragement) with which we ourselves are comforted (consoled and encouraged) by God.
2 Corinthians 1:3–4 (AMPCE)

January 9

"Get out of the boat" faith—that's what I desire! I want to be like Peter! Yes, he floundered at times. But when it came to taking a step of faith for the Lord, he jumped right in with both feet.

The scenario: Peter sees Jesus walking on the water. The other disciples watch in fear and awe as they witness their Master surfing the waves—without a surfboard. Peter, seemingly without hesitation, asks, "May I come to you?" Jesus says yes, and Peter goes out to him.

Sure, he sank. Yet Peter got out of the boat. That same boldness is what carried Peter through very challenging times for a Christian. In the end, the same Peter who denied Jesus three times, was crucified for his faith. He loved God enough to suggest, "If I am to die, I will die. Yet I am not fit to die in the same way as my Lord." So Peter was crucified upside down because he was forever sold out for Jesus!

My desire is to have a heart like Peter. Lord, help us to be sold out for You. Impart in us the fearlessness to stand for Your Word, Your way for this life. Thank You, Jesus, for forging the way for us. We love You, Lord.

January 10

Recently I heard a pastor preaching about the "exceptional" people of God.

And it is true that, as Christians, we are not an ordinary people, because our God is not ordinary. We are set apart because our Lord is extraordinary. But that is not to say we should be prideful, or believe we are better than others. Our quest is to be a shining, but humble example of Jesus's love.

This sermon on exceptionalism of God's people was not resonating in my spirit. I asked God, "Why?" God spoke to my heart that the preacher was asking people to say to each other, "I am exceptional." The Lord further said to me, "My people should say to each other, 'You are exceptional!'"

You see, we must always strive to lift others up and not ourselves. This is the true vision of Jesus Christ. Jesus was humble. Yet He was the Son of God. His goal was to continually help others. We should never be the focus. Jesus should be the focus.

I heard another minister say, "When a Christian walks into church, they should say, 'There you are,' not 'Here I am.'"

Love is patient and kind; love does not envy or boast; it is not arrogant or rude. It does not insist on its own way; it is not irritable or resentful; it does not rejoice at wrongdoing, but rejoices with the truth. Love bears all things, believes all things, hopes all things, endures all things. Love never ends.
1 Corinthians 13:4–8 (ESV)

January 11

True God-given faith is
Being convinced of,
No matter what,
God will do this,
He's got your back.
Sometimes all we see,
Is the storm is raging,
The sky is hazy, Life is crazy.
It is not over, He is God.
No matter what, Life is hard.
Believing costs nothing,
But He is the One thing
That pulls you through.
Soon we will see living proof
Of what our God can do.
He is the light in the night,
He is the courage in the fight.
He is our past, present, and future tense
Where He is, we are our best.
Who knows,
What our future holds.
In the hands of God,
This mustard seed pod
Faith grows and
Nothing's too hard.

January 12

One morning, during my commute to work, I had a "God" experience! In my quest for human perfection (lol), I realized that God's realm is outside the box, and in Him, there is no formula or equation to figure out. More than prayer, God desires a relationship with Him!

Once inside my vehicle that day, I set my sights to pray. Just then, a song came on the radio, which was one I knew. Suddenly, I realized within the lyrics of the song, I was having communion with the Lord of the universe. At that moment, the heartfelt words of Steven Curtis Chapman brought me to be one with God.

It was not prayer, but true intimacy with the Lord that brought me joy. This is not to say God does not want us to pray. But God's ultimate desire is communication and intimacy with His kids.

Let us be open to the voice of our Lord, moment to moment, day to day. He is yearning for a private meeting with Him.

January 13

I feel the breath of life spring forth,
I sense it is time to grow,
I must ascend to a higher course,
Where living waters flow.
The climb may take a rocky turn,
But God will see me through,
He gives me hind's feet, swift and sure,
I'll not be tripped or moved.
His well, my source of strength awaits,
To quench, when I must drink,
He takes me from the earthen clay,
To the rock, so I won't sink.
When a storm is drawing near,
I hide beneath the cleft,
The load is light enough to bear,
Under His wings, He gives me rest.
The sun's hot rays won't scorch or hurt,
In the shadow of His love.
His refuge waits at every turn,
His grace, much more than enough.
My destiny, His secret place,
His glory greets me there,
In quiet, I am warm and safe,
I speak to God in prayer.

January 14

Social media is at its peak in today's society. Many people give a great deal of attention and time to Facebook and Twitter. I myself enjoy daily posts from friends, as well as reading the many articles. Many people share pictures of others, or take selfies to post. It was when I noticed one of those selfies that God impressed upon my heart why so many are desperately looking to impress others.

The Lord was not being condemning when He also placed upon my heart, "I want you all to learn to impress me. It is My delight that you desire to seek My face."

God is so patient and kind with His children. He extends His grace to us all. When we are out of balance, He beckons us back kindly and gently. He wants us to enjoy life. But He also wants us to daily seek His awesome presence.

Take delight in the LORD, and he will give you the desires

of your heart.

Psalm 37:4 (NIV)

January 15

I am flawed, God is not.

In my earnest desire to put out a spark, I start a fire.

While reaching for things I want, I overlook the important
thoughts.

It is the journey that is important, not the destination.

I hurt, I bruise, I inflict pain on others too.

We are all guilty of small and large wars. Because of these,
we have battle scars.

Our God is sufficient for every pain,

The cross covers every wound we create.

It also soothes all hurts and scars.

Jesus restores broken hearts.

Thank You, Lord, for making us clean,

He would do it again, just for you and me.

For God so loved the world, that He gave His only
perish, but have eternal life. For God did not send the Son
into the world to judge the world, but that the world might
be saved through Him.
John 3:16–17 (NASB)

January 16

Deep within the earth's surface, with extreme heat and pressure, a diamond is made. With the gradual shifting of the earth's plates and volcanic eruptions, it is brought near the surface. Then, only in the hands of a master craftsman, can this rock-like substance be transformed to a magnificently shaped diamond. The purposeful blows with a hammer, the chiseling, with precision and expertise, brings beauty from blah.

Likewise, God is continually chiseling and molding us into what He has created us to be. At times, the pressure is intense. The heat can sometimes be more than we think we can bear. But the Master Craftsman is very purposeful in working with His creation. He wants us to be someone worthy of His stamp of approval. He is not concerned about the imperfections He trims away. He sees the finished work. He sees us as the brilliant diamond, long before we see it.

And yet, O LORD, You are our Father. We are the clay, and you are the potter. We all are formed by your hand.

Isaiah 64:8 (NLT)

January 17

My God shall supply all your need according to His riches

in glory by Jesus Christ.

Philippians 4:19 (NKJV)

It has taken me many years (and I am still learning) to realize I do not have to carry the weight of the world on my shoulders. I thought it was my job to worry about money, family, and everything else. I was so consumed by worrying about money, I often had dreams about my purse being stolen or lost. God showed me that the root of being overly concerned about finances and other things is never feeling safe. Deep down, I was always fearful I would be left alone, without anyone to depend on.

Through the healing process, God has shown me that I can totally depend and lean on Him. He is our safe harbor in the night. In the shadows, He is the light. He will never leave us, or forsake us. I can say that now with confidence, as He has proven His love again and again.

You can always count on Jesus.

January 18

As sure as we take our next breath, persecution will come. We live in a fallen world where we all sin and fall short of the glory of God. But the Bible says to put on the armor of God to fight evil when it comes.

What is the armor? The belt of truth. The helmet of salvation. The breastplate of righteousness. The shield of faith. The sword of the Spirit. Our feet shod with the preparation of the gospel. (See Ephesians 6:10–18.)

The Bible promises that the earnest, heartfelt prayer of a righteous person makes tremendous power available (James 5:16b).

How do we become righteous?

No other way than going to the cross of Jesus. The blood of the Lamb and the word of our testimony in combination is the strongest weapon on earth to fight persecution. You see, on our own, we are weak. But with God, we are strong in the Lord and in the power of His might—because "If God be for us, who can be against us?" (Romans 8:31b KJV).

Rejoice that we are overcomers by Jesus Christ!

January 19

Surviving life's storms may not be a matter of taking giant leaps and bounds, but rather being consistent through each day—praying through the torrential downpour until we safely arrive at our destination.

Although there are many trials to overcome, we become victors when we know God is steadfast and faithful in helping us to be overcomers. However, even more so, God desires for us to thrive through the desert seasons of our lives, rather than just survive.

He will support us no matter how we walk through the desert, though. But His hope is that we run the race as one who knows they have the victory from the start. That is what faith in the power of God does. That is what "blessed assurance" is—belief in the One who makes miracles happen.

January 20

In the time of a sweet,

Sweet second,

We will have a revelation,

And nothing is the same,

When we realize His grace.

At the moment

our eyes have opened,

We can see the path before us;

With clarity, awareness,

He creates a light to lead us.

What best describes this "glory,"

While I stumbled in clay, miry,

Then He sent

A light my way,

You, my Lord created "day."

Light arises in the darkness for the upright, gracious,

compassionate, and just [who are in right standing with

God]. Psalm 112:4

January 21

I am not yet where I want to be. But I know God is never finished with me!

Knowing who we are in Christ and confessing the Word will bring us out of the miry clay and plant us on the rock.

When we know how much He loves us, we know God is Love! He can be nothing else (see 1 John 4:7–21). Through communion with God, His love is brought to full completion. It is a perfect love. No other love can and will ever compare.

His love is patient and will not force us to do His will. But when we walk out of God's will, we will stumble and fall. It is up to us to repent and go back to God. He will always be waiting. You see, He never leaves our side. It is we who walk away.

Yet He welcomes us back with open arms, tossing our iniquities into the sea of forgetfulness, never to be seen again. His Word assures us that if we are seeking first the kingdom and His righteousness, all things will be given unto us (Matthew 6:33).

Thank you, Lord, for all Your wondrous gifts. We are blessed beyond measure by Your perfect love. Help us to better comprehend Your love and to be a living example of it by walking in it every day.

In Jesus's Name. Amen

January 22

I feel battered, quite tattered, and torn,
Thoughts scattered, unmattered, and worn.
But there's a thorn
In the crown of a Prince of Peace,
Who was beaten and scorn
For the scars and grief,
He has taken it all to the cross for you and me,
And they hung our King,
There, between 2 thieves,
This is our battle cry,
Our renowned relief.
God said, You don't have to die!
But He did it all for you and I.
That Jesus Christ,
He went all the way,
To hell and back,
Beyond the grave.
He took the keys
To set us free.
Evil concedes,
Death has no sting.
Let's stand and believe,
Whatever the battle,
Our victory is through
The One who matters.

January 23

Let us proclaim today that we have the victory! This is not to say we will not encounter trials and adversity, but we are boldly confessing, "No longer will trials overtake me!"

An example is when Jesus and the apostles were in a boat one day, and a violent storm approached and the men feared for their lives. Jesus continued to rest in the storm until the apostles woke Him because they were so afraid. Jesus rebuked them by saying, "Why are you timid and afraid, O you of little faith?" (Matthew 8:26 AMPCE).

Just as Jesus awoke and rebuked the wind, we must awake from our complacency to address the situations in our lives. Jesus spoke to the storm, "Shalom, be still!"

As we saw in the reading for January 6, the word *"shalom"* means "peace." But the original Hebrew text meaning of this common greeting is to be safe, be well, be happy, have health, have prosperity, as well as to be at peace. I would say that just about covers everything!

I am the vine, you are the branches. He who abides in Me,
and I in him, bears much fruit; for without Me you can do
nothing.
John 15:5 (NKJV)

January 24

"Me and my big mouth!" So many times in my walk with the Lord, I have spoken, or thought this. You see, there are many references in the Bible, which speak about the words of our mouth. Here are two of them for you:

Death and life are in the power of the tongue, and those who love it will eat its fruit. Proverbs 18:21 (nkjv)

For by your words you will be acquitted, and by your words you will be condemned. Matthew 12:37 (niv)

How about negativity? "I dislike that person. ... This is never going to work. ... I hate my job." These are only a few examples of the things we say every day.

I am passing it on to you now. You have a challenge as a child of God to speak words of life, not death. Do not get discouraged if you make mistakes. Jesus has your back. Just try, and God will do the rest!

So also the tongue is a small part of the body, and yet it boasts of great things. See how great a forest is set aflame by such a small fire! And the tongue is a fire, the very world of iniquity; the tongue is set among our members as that which defiles the entire body, and sets on fire the course of our life, and is set on fire by he. James 3:5–6 (nasb)

January 25

One day my thoughts were focused on a dear person whose husband departed from this earth way too soon. He fought a long and hard battle with cancer. He left behind a legacy of two children and a wife who planned to have him for her "happily ever after."

How does one bring comfort to soothe the heart that breaks?

It does not seem fair to witness a young life snuffed out. Life sometimes can be gut-wrenching. We've all been dealt the hand of death and loss. We want to be comforted and to give comfort. We want to heal and see healing.

I have found the best comfort for these times are not in words, but actions: a hug, a shoulder to cry on and to lean on. A gift of time spent together can soothe much better than all the words in the dictionary.

Rest in the knowledge that with the same love given to us by Jesus, it is passed on through us as we comfort one another.

Blessed be the God and Father of our Lord Jesus Christ, the Father of mercies and God of all comfort, who comforts us in all our affliction, so that we may be able to comfort those who are in any affliction, with the comfort with which we ourselves are comforted by God. For as we share abundantly in Christ's sufferings, so through Christ we share abundantly in comfort too.

2 Corinthians 1:3–5 (ESV)

January 26

One winter's day came very close to being "The day from
hell." On my commute to work, I got stuck in the snow
twice. There I was, helpless, spinning my tires, near the top
of a hill. Grrrr. I grumbled. I moaned. Then I just said,
"Jesus, help me."

Just then, against the odds, I began making
progress. It didn't come instantly. But eventually I was able
to make it to the top of the hill.

Soon, another hill, and I was stuck again. With
several cars behind me, I suddenly decided to turn around
and take another route.

I arrived at work forty-five minutes late. But I
arrived, safe and sound.

Thank You, God, for sticking with me. I know the

trouble I can be.

January 27

Happy are those who trust in the Lord with their whole heart and lean not on their own understanding!

God was very purposeful in bringing manna to the people of Israel daily (see Exodus 16). Those who tried to store it away for later soon realized it became spoiled and not fit for consumption. The next day, the Lord brought fresh manna for the people as they trusted Him for provision.

Likewise, the Bible teaches us to not trust in earthly goods and possessions that will soon corrode and rust. But value and trust in the eternal God of our salvation, who will never disappoint, nor turn us away.

It is easy to believe for provision when the job provides pay, the money is in the bank, and the food is in the refrigerator. The challenge comes when we lose the job, our funds are exhausted, and the fridge is empty.

It is in the hard times that our faith in God for provision needs to be exercised.

Standing on God's Word to supply our every need according to His riches in glory through Christ Jesus carries us through the challenging times until God's manna manifests in our lives. (See Philippians 4:19.)

January 28

We go through so many seasons in our lives, some of which we do not understand. There are natural times of planting, dormancy, and harvesting. Many times we question the reasons for the seasons. To our human minds, it makes no sense.

But through our spiritual eyes, we have the potential to see God contriving a wonderful symphony that He is orchestrating through us all.

It is through these many seasons we will find growth, love, and acceptance to life's most challenging questions. It is then we will find true peace in God and with ourselves.

To everything there is a season, a time for every purpose

under heaven.

Ecclesiastes 3:1 (NKJV)

January 29

In the stillness of Your glory,
I see the goodness of Your ways,
I see myself enduring,
Though the storms may come my way.
I've exchanged my strength for Your strength,
I am covered by Your love,
Your mercy, it sustains me,
Though the going may get rough.
I see the path ahead now,
Your brilliance lights my way.
I am calmed by Your lovely heart sounds,
I'm secure in Your strong embrace.
Life's troubles, they are fleeting,
What is now, will soon be gone,
But God's love is ever with me,
Through His presence, I stand strong.

Now to Him Who, by (in consequence of) the [action of His] power that is at work within us, is able to [carry out His purpose and] do superabundantly, far over and above all that we [dare] ask or think [infinitely beyond our highest prayers, desires, thoughts, hopes, or dreams] ...
Ephesians 3:20 (AMPCE)

January 30

Before He left the earth, Jesus said, "I will not leave you orphans" (John 14:18 NKJV). The King James Version renders it, "I will not leave you comfortless." In fulfillment of this promise, Jesus sent the Holy Spirit, the Comforter, the one called alongside of us, our aide and advocate. We are not alone!

We may sometimes feel isolated in our circumstances. This is a way the enemy uses to cause us to feel despair. Separation, isolation, and insulation is counterproductive to growing in God. When times are hard and you are feeling hopeless, just reach out to God. He will bring positive people into your life, those who will encourage you and strengthen you through the tough trials of life.

Proverbs 27:17 (NKJV) says, "As iron sharpens iron, so a man sharpens the countenance of his friend."

Remember, you are not alone!

January 31

I was a little behind on my commute to work one morning. So my usual stop for iced tea at the coffee place was hurried, and thus I sped up to the drive-thru lane. Then I saw a man sitting to my right, waiting to merge into the waiting line-up of vehicles.

Should I let him in? ... I'm running late! ... I was here before him! ... were my thoughts.

I heard a gentle whisper, "Let him go."

A moment later, I let the man pull into the line in front of me.

I got up to the window, and the girl said with a smile, "That gentleman paid for your tea."

That kind gesture made my day and brought tears to my eyes. It was more than a drink. It was a wink from God.

February 1

In a twinkling of an eye, everything can change! Used to describe how quickly we will be transported to heaven in 1 Corinthians 15:52, a "twinkling of an eye" is about eleven one-hundredths of a second, according to scientists.

It is inconceivable how quickly God can work! He truly has the power to transform any situation, no matter how dismal it seems, into a life-giving, hopeful, praise-filled breakthrough! I recently had a miracle, and I know with all my heart that it was God who caused it to happen for me. After a series of disappointments, I sat in my car and God said, "Just praise Me and thank Me."

In a quiet whisper, with no enthusiasm whatsoever, I started to praise and thank God for everything I have. With tears streaming down my face, I realized I am blessed! I went home and thought, *I am going to give back to God, not out of lack, but out of gratitude.* I gave an extra donation to Billy Graham ministries, and I felt so good doing it. I didn't think about what I did not have; I thought about how much God has blessed me.

The next day, I had a major miracle in my finances. I tell you, God's Word is true. It says, "Give, and it will be given to you: good measure, pressed down, shaken together, and running over will be put into your bosom" (Luke 6:38 NKJV).

February 2

From the pit to the palace! In the book of Genesis, Joseph suffered one adversity after another. In reading about his life, one would be amazed that he never threw in the towel.

His jealous brothers threw him into a pit and sold him into slavery. After being sold in Egypt, he rose up and gained a good standing in Potiphar's house—until Potiphar's wife made advances toward Joseph. When Joseph refused, Potiphar's wife lied and said Joseph tried to attack her. Joseph was thrown into prison.

He stayed there for a couple of years until the day came when he was called by Pharaoh to interpret his disturbing dreams. Joseph found favor with the king. But he struggled through difficult times from the age of seventeen until he was thirty, when he finally saw a breakthrough in his life.

One key element resounds throughout Joseph's walk: he never gave up.

It may seem like things will never go your way, but God will never disappoint you—or give up on you.

Faithful is He who calls you, and He also will bring it to pass.
1 Thessalonians 5:24 (NASB)

February 3

The glory of the Lord endures forever!

As I am reading Psalm 27, my heart leaps for joy in the knowledge of the power and goodness of our God! Though we may be in the throes of trouble and affliction, we have great hope that God will prevail and we will certainly overcome.

Take heart, my beautiful friends, for this season will surely pass. You have blessed assurance that God will not forget you.

"Weeping may endure for the night, but joy comes in the morning" (Psalm 30:5 NKJV). These wonderful words from God's own Spirit are an eternal contract, signed with the indelible blood of Christ. No power on earth or in hell can make us exempt from receiving His promises, unless we exclude ourselves.

"Ye are of God, little children, and have overcome them: because greater is he that is in you, than he that is in the world" (1 John 4:4 KJV). Therefore, let us rejoice, as the battle has been fought and won, and through Jesus, we are indeed victorious!

February 4

The journey was long and hard. But a prodigal daughter found her way home to Jesus. The particulars (who, what, where) about this story are not relevant.

Life had taken many twists and turns. God's strongest soldiers endure the toughest battles, after all. She had already started attending a church near her home. But she desired to visit her old church, from back when she was a little girl.

She seemed to yearn for a familiar, safe haven to help her on this new journey. As she conveyed her experience, I saw such a deep sadness in her eyes. She expressed great disappointment in what the pastor had shared, as the message had focused on some building fund. She yearned for a word that would bring her back home, with new strength to carry on.

Many are more concerned today about the building of the church structure, rather than bringing the news that we are the church of Christ.

We are more than bricks and mortar. We are His living epistles.

Let us be a beacon of hope to those who are searching for the light of Jesus Christ.

February 5

I take your hand gently in Mine,
Your smile so real, I can see your heart,
I see Myself in your soft eyes.
I see how the years have brought you hurt,
But I see past all those signs;
I only see what you deserve.
I dance to the beat of your heartstrings,
I follow your lead as we twirl;
I smile as you sing in my ear.
I caress your heart
And healing comes.
I love you, little girl.
We don't need to talk,
Our language transcends words,
I hear your mind whispering,
"Once more, Jesus, once more."
Do not worry, my child,
This dance goes on and on,
Let us dance now in your dreams,
To the Spirit's own sweet song.

The Lord is my Strength and Song; and He has become my

Salvation.

Psalm 118:14 (AMPCE)

February 6

I once saw a powerful testimony of a woman who was healed of a terrible disease. She went to her church and had everyone pray for her. But she said the breakthrough came when she felt God say to her, "You will be healed when you give thanks to Me."

At first the woman thought, *How do I give thanks for this suffering?*

Then she remembered 1 Thessalonians 5:18 (KJV)— "In every thing give thanks: for this is the will of God in Christ Jesus concerning you."

She began thanking God with her whole heart for helping her get through another day. She thanked Him for the strength in her body to walk a step. Suddenly she felt she was healed. She immediately told her husband and children and they all rejoiced for her healing.

This woman received her healing because she took a step of faith, being thankful in all things. No we do not thank God for the disease, condition, or situation. God did not create these things. We thank Him for the every little detail that causes us to get through another moment.

At that time Jesus answered and said, I thank thee, O Father, Lord of heaven and earth, because thou hast hid these things from the wise and prudent, and hast revealed them unto babes.
Matthew 11:25 (KJV)

February 7

God is the great "I AM," not the "I was" or the "I will be." His magnificence always centers in the here and now.

We can take a cue from our flawless Father and not dwell upon the past failures, hurts, and regrets. It will not change a single thing, but will rather affect our present being.

Also, worrying about the future is not living in God's best interest for His children. This attitude of dread brings on a spirit of fear that will attach itself, never willing to let go. The Bible says, "God has not given us a spirit of fear, but of power and of love and of a sound mind" (2 Timothy 1:7 NKJV).

The Word of God also references the birds of the air and the lilies of the field—how they neither toil nor spin (worry). Yet God takes care of them. How much more are we to God than these? (See Matthew 6:26–30.)

I don't know about you, but this truly gives me comfort to know my God is ever present and more than capable of handling all that concerns me.

"My God shall supply all your need according to His riches in glory by Christ Jesus" (Philippians 4:19 NKJV). Alleluia!

February 8

One day, as I was using my iPhone to direct me to a new
destination, I learned a valuable lesson.
While going to an unfamiliar part of town, I started the
drive from the place I knew would take me to the general
vicinity. This was not the designated route the navigator
was taking me on.

But as soon as the system was aware I was taking
another way, it adapted and redirected, using the current
location.

Wouldn't it be great if we could adjust to changes in
life as easily as that? The twists and turns of daily living
can be quite unsettling. Many times our expectations are to
go one way, and life re-routes us. Disappointment and
heartache follow when our hopes are dashed. But as we
walk with the Lord, we can rely on the Holy Spirit to lead
and guide us into all truth. Jesus left us with the comforter,
the one called alongside us, so that we would not feel
"stranded" in life. We can go our way with confidence,
knowing the Lord will direct our steps. If we get lost, don't
worry; God will always find us.

February 9

God told me to tell you that you are going to make it through this dark hour.

Never mind the past times that devastated you and held your peace for ransom.

Just keep your focus on His Word, and He will carry you through this season effortlessly.

He is surely able to provide for your every need.

So, do not waste your time worrying, beloved.

Just give it all over to Him and He will carry you over to the other side.

I lift my eyes to the mountains—where does my help come from? My help comes from the Lord, the maker of Heaven and earth.

Psalm 121:1-2 (NIV)

February 10

Draw near to God and He will draw near to you.

James 4:8 (NASB)

God waits for us to make the first move. You see, He is a gracious Father who gives His children room. As soon as we say, "Hello Father," we have His undivided attention. You can be sure of it. He does not hold us to formalities. He is not staunch, or stiff. We need only to just be "us."

Not to worry if you do not have the words. Sometimes "Help, Lord" will suffice. Give Him a moment, or more if you can. He is willing and eager to listen. The one who holds all our tomorrows in His hands, wants to hear from you today.

February 11

Lord Jesus, help us to draw near to You in these turbulent times. Many things are happening in this world, which can cause us to shrink back in terror. With Your Spirit and Your Word in us, we have the potential to resist fear.

Help us to go to Your Word and glean the necessary tools to stave off the arrows of evil.

Jesus, we thank You for Your precious blood that empowers us for the battle!

Victory is imminent in Jesus!

February 12

Sometimes I feel like I'm floating
On a wing and a prayer,
Life can seem willy-nilly,
As if we're alone out here.
But I know You are with me,
You are standing right beside me.
When the water's getting deep,
I cannot hold on,
You give me the strength I need,
I will keep on going.
Fear has me frozen,
In its agonizing grip,
I will ascend the steepest terrain,
You will never let me slip.
You say, "Do not be afraid,
I am with you," and You smile,
You chase all the fears away,
I can rest with You now.
My heart may be racing,
My feet may be pacing,
Inside I am weeping,
I will not let it defeat me.
You are God;
This I know: You will never let me go.

February 13

*Surely He has borne our griefs (sicknesses, weaknesses,
and distresses) and carried our sorrows and pains [of
punishment], yet we [ignorantly] considered Him stricken,
smitten, and afflicted by God [as if with leprosy]. But He
was wounded for our transgressions, He was bruised for
our guilt and iniquities; the chastisement [needful to
obtain] peace and well-being for us was upon Him, and
with the stripes [that wounded] Him we are healed and
made whole.*
Isaiah 53:4–5 (AMPCE)

Lord, with Your light comes awareness. Awareness means
tending to inward emotions, so one can effectively deal
with outside surroundings. Although feelings cannot be
seen in the physical sense, they shape the way one views
the outward environment. Allowing God in essentially
means to allow His light in to envelop the dark places. Only
then are we able to clear out the mind and deal with any
pain, grief, and bitterness hidden in secret.

Remain fixed on God to carry you through the
rough patches. Bring all emotions to the feet of Jesus so He
can carry the burden. Painful memories, like dust, will
transform a shiny, new surface into a dull, worn-looking
exterior unless awareness is maintained. A lifelong change
begins one step at a time.

February 14

Today is a day of celebrating love. We often think of Valentine's Day as an occasion for sweethearts and romance. But this morning I awoke to the thoughts of a Creator who brought love into existence. Without Him, we would know no love. The most famous Bible verse begins, "For God so loved the world" that He gave a Savior, that we would not perish, but have everlasting life (John 3:16). It is difficult to comprehend the enormity of that kind of love.

Each one of us is loved with the intensity of life and death.

Bottom line: He was born to die so that we could love, live, and have the ultimate promise of a home in heaven.

Jesus, You are our one true valentine!

February 15

Listen for the sound of God's voice. It most always is not audible. But it is evident in the transformation of our circumstances, and the affirmation of love from a friend, family, or even a complete stranger.

It may seem so coincidental that you could miss it. Like the day I was crying out in my car, "Lord, do You hear me?" I glanced up and the bumper sticker on the car in front of me read, "Jesus loves you."

He will give His answer. It may not be instantaneous. But if you wait and rest in the stillness of your faith, He will transform your life to better suit His peace (*shalom*) and ultimately yours.

I now realize the things I asked for in the past may have eclipsed my world, and thereby affected my relationship with God. He knows what we can handle, whether it be material things, relationships, or vocations. You may think hitting the lottery won't change you one bit, but He can see where it would take you.

He hears your voice, your cries, your whispers.

And at times, instead of granting our requests, He transforms our dreams to align with our best interests.

Sometimes He will shift the paradigm to save our life, or our eternal souls.

One thing I am sure of: Father knows best.

February 16

"Stick with Me, the best is yet to come!"

The Lord is saying to you this day,

I know you've heard empty promises and experienced

many disappointments in the past. But I am your God and

not a man that I should lie.

I will stand with you and hold you up when you can no

longer support yourself.

You are not meant to do life alone. That is why you feel so

tired.

Take my Word upon you, for they that wait upon Me shall

have their strength renewed.

You will walk and not grow weary. You will run and not

faint.

If you exchange your strength for Mine, I will empower

you for future challenges.

Do not be afraid for me to take charge.

Through your God, you will do mighty exploits.

Nothing is impossible to those who place their trust in Me.

February 17

In walking the road to freedom, adversity is guaranteed to come (see John 16:33). We have all let ourselves be devastated by affliction in the past. Now when troubles rear their ugly head and we feel overwhelmed, sometimes all we can muster up is "Jesus!" And that's a good thing!

There is power in the name of Jesus. The Bible says that in the name of Jesus, every knee must bow and every tongue confess that He is Lord (Philippians 2:9–11).

When sadness comes, it must bow to the name of Jesus.

When sickness comes, it must concede to Jesus.

Anger must relinquish its power in the mighty name of Jesus.

Jesus has the authority over all heaven and earth. He stilled the storms and the ferocious waves obeyed at the sound of His voice.

He is the same God today as He was then, and He will silence the tempests of your life. When you don't know what to say, just say "Jesus!"

February 18

As soon as the sun reached its place on the horizon, the clouds in all their brilliance spilled over in the western sky, echoing hues of fuchsia and violet.

Moments later, I witnessed the beauty dissipate as the sun hid itself from the day. The clouds were brought to darkness, without color or substance.

I thought, *It is the light from the sun, reflecting through objects, that transforms the mundane.*

How very true it can be said with the Son of God also. Until the Son shines through us, with all His brilliance, we are mere mortals living in existence. The spirit is dark, the soul colorless, as one lacks Him who brings light out of darkness.

But the beauty comes just as soon as we invite the Son in. Jesus, without hesitation, illuminates every dingy part of our beings. We are transformed by His presence. We now reflect His radiance.

We have forever become children of the light!

February 19

The time spent in this valley
Is but a temporary trial,
I walked the rugged, steep terrain,
I will walk another mile.
The rushing torrent of the water
Tries to engulf me with its waves,
The mighty hand of God holds on
To bring me where I'm safe.
Scaling the mountainous regions ahead
Feels challenging at times,
Not knowing what's around the bend,
I am going through this blind.
But God as navigator
Charts out a perfect way,
He knows exactly where to lead,
I won't be led astray.
He gives me clarity of thought,
I choose the right decisions,
There is no fear of tomorrow,
God has assured me His provision.
Every day of life I'm blessed,
No matter where I am,
In the valley or the mountaintop,
On His solid rock I stand.

February 20

Recently in my daily travels, I observed an automatic lawn sprinkler gone awry. Its job was to water a piece of a beautifully landscaped lawn. It obviously malfunctioned, as it was watering only the road and the vehicles that passed by it.

As I sat there waiting for the light to change, I thought, *What a great waste of resources!*

Then the Lord brought to my attention how we do this every day.

In our aim and desire to get things done, we sometimes overlook God's grander scheme of things. We miss the proverbial forest through His trees. "Watering" in the eyes of God may mean taking the time to help someone while carrying out a daily task. The words "May I help you?" can be thirst quenching to someone who is traveling through a desert experience of life.

Wasteful watering is utilizing our God-given abilities and resources only on "me and mine." If we can only cast our sights beyond our own front lawns, we will see a world in need. If they can find Jesus through us, they will discover the endless source of refreshment, from whom they can continually drink.

February 21

Jesus explained to me, "I know you do not like rocking the boat. But consider this: sometimes in your earnest desire to be compliant and not make waves, the boat rocks you!"

Many people will be angry or offended at the stance we take for the Lord. But this is our mission if we are to be His followers.

In the words of Jesus: "Therefore everyone who confesses Me before men, I will also confess him before My Father who is in heaven. But whoever denies Me before men, I will also deny him before My Father who is in heaven" (Matthew 10:32 NASB).

Life at times can be like a storm that rages with the opposition of those who want to silence the voices of God's people.

We will fight, not in anger. But in love and with assurance, knowing the battle is the Lord's.

Fighting the "good fight of faith" mentioned in 1 Timothy 6:12 (NASB) sometimes means you need to speak out for God when you would rather be silent, or holding your tongue when your flesh wants you to verbally rip into someone.

It is a matter of letting the Lord lead. We can be assured of one thing: they will hate us as they hated Him.

You will be hated by all because of My name, but it is the one who has endured to the end who will be saved.
Matthew 10:21–22 (NASB)

February 22

The day will come when everyone—believers, nonbelievers, and those who are lukewarm—will have to give an account of their life before almighty God.

I would rather disappoint countless men than do the same to my heavenly Father. Yes, I want people to like me. But most of all, when I reach heaven, I want God to say, "Well done, good and faithful servant!"

You see, Jesus's main goal is to feed His sheep. He asked Peter, "Do you love me? Then feed my sheep." (See John 21:15–17.)

God does not want us to go out on the streets, screaming "Repent! The kingdom of God is near!" He wants us to take His message of love to whatever forum He sends us and never stop!

Let us be relentless in our goal of pleasing God, rather than pleasing man.

February 23

One of the most challenging things in life is doing the right thing when everything around us seems to be going wrong.

When our world appears as though it is coming apart at the seams, when all that we believed for has seemingly fallen apart, remember that God is not finished yet.

You've stayed the course. You've tried to remain strong in the Lord. Sure, you have stumbled from time to time. But haven't we all?

So when will the promise be fulfilled? Why all the adversity still?

God's Word promises that "He is a rewarder of those who diligently seek Him" (Hebrews 11:6 NKJV).

Sometimes our diligence—persistent, hardworking effort—requires us to keep on keeping on for years. What is it all about? You may think, *Is God torturing me?*

Nothing of the sort! God is continually orchestrating our lives in such a way that we will have no other option but to believe that He is responsible for the results.

He makes a way where there seems to be none. When all looks lost, He will shine a beacon of light to bring you home. Even though it looks as though dreams have been shattered, He will mend the broken pieces and create a treasure better than you could have imagined.

February 24

Whenever the world is finished with you, you will always
  have Jesus!
You've burned every proverbial bridge, and your remnants
  of a last chance scatter like the wind. But He will
  always be there to gather the pieces.
When the darkness lay with you at night, making it known
  it will be your strange, constant bedfellow, He shatters
  the ebony shroud and the sun breaks through.
Oh wretched human that I am! Who will Love me when I
  am the least loveable?
Jesus will!
He peels back the layers of dirt, the pollution of humanity,
  and rescues your heart in the midst of the rubble.
He wipes every tear, soothes every fear, and answers every
  prayer.
Your empty promises to Him fell along the wayside,
  leaving you feeling hopeless and disappointed.
But Jesus just smiles and says, "I will take care of you."
His Love is relentless. His gaze? Limitless.
You can hide in the deepest, darkest cavern of misery and
  He will find you.

If your life thus far, has played out like a pitiful novel at the
five-and-dime store,
He will give you a new day, a new story, and a new song in
   your heart.
Before my Jesus, mediocre was my finest hour. But now
   my yesteryears of bitter sorrow only serve as a gauge of
   how far I've come.
I am not prideful, but I boast in the Savior's great exploits
   in my being.
I was once a lump of dirty coal. But Jesus made a diamond
   out of me.
Your journey is over! It has just begun!
Let God navigate your life's course.
You will never be the same!

February 25

Love was born at Christmas.

On Easter, Love was transformed, empowered, and
deposited in each one of us.

The same Love that brought Jesus to the cross, dwells in us.

The power of Love that never ends, that sets the captives
free, that brings us from hell to the streets of gold, it
lives on!

It is up to us to spread the Word. Love is alive!

Jesus is our Gift of Love and He never turns anyone away.

His sacrifice ensured everyone's entrance into the kingdom,

Unlike Jesus who was despised and rejected.

He will never say, "You are a loser!"

Our Savior is the ultimate Friend. He is the original "Love
Story."

February 26

I had it, but I thought I lost it.

I went in the opposite direction.

He didn't run from me though,

I ran from him.

He didn't want me to go.

He wanted me to stop and listen.

I know now, he loves me so much. He wants the very best

for me. But sometimes I don't believe the very best is for

me.

I looked to other resources for my hope and my happiness

and at those times it didn't work. If it felt good, it was

short-lived, and not real, honest to God peace.

But He is very real.

He takes the messes of our lives and weeds out everything

that's not good, and plants what is needful and beautiful.

We give Him the worst and He makes the best out of it.

That is just his way. "Beauty for ashes."

He knows what's best because he is the best!

On both good and bad days, I think about that!

February 27

When I sit and ponder the journey that Mary and Joseph took before the birth of Jesus, I am in awe of the wonder of it all. Theirs was more than a physical pilgrimage; it was a journey of overcoming obstacles that were insurmountable in their society.

Mary was pledged to Joseph. As was customary, a woman remained with her family for one year following her betrothal until she was joined with her husband.

Shortly after the engagement, Mary was visited by the angel and she became pregnant with the Son of God. Joseph, who later found her to be with child, desired to break the engagement. But, shortly afterward, he received word through a dream that Mary was carrying the Messiah in her womb.

Imagine the implications when word hit the streets: Mary was carrying a bastard child—and the outcome could have been bleak.

What proved to be providential for the couple was a call for a census. All citizens had to report to their place of origin to be included in the census. Joseph was from Bethlehem, which was one hundred miles away. He and Mary left behind all the sneers and jeers of the people who persecuted them and set off on their journey.

They were very poor and had very little to take with them. But in spite of the opposition they knew lay ahead, they held on to the miracle Mary carried inside her.

They knew they were poor, they knew they were scorned, they realized the journey was long. But they held on to the dream.

Now the Miracle lives and He resides in all who believe.

In spite of whatever opposition, adversity, slander, poverty, and sickness we encounter, we know He lives and He is working on behalf of us all.

We are all on a journey. But we are never alone in our trials.

Jesus has assured us in His Word that He will never leave us. He is always as close as our heart, and He is working to complete the miracle that lives on in each of us.

This is His gift to us: His never-ending quest to give us His very best.

February 28

One of the most challenging things for me is to allow God to navigate my way in life. Even though I know He knows the best way to go, I still have a tendency to try to control the issues I am concerned about.

When God placed it upon my heart to share His Word on a certain Facebook group, I had the nerve to ask, "Are You sure you want me to do this?"

Imagine God saying, "Um, actually, no ... I am not positive." lol

As I share these devotionals with you, I want you to know how humbled I am to be in this position. I am quite imperfect; I feel at times I am hopelessly flawed. But it does not matter how I feel. What matters most is obedience to God.

I could not be here solely based on my qualifications. I have none. But God does not call the qualified. He qualifies the called. He gives me the words to share with you daily—fresh manna.

It is His love for you that causes Him to share the word. He wants us to hope. He desires us to place our hopes in Him. If we trust in Him, He will not disappoint!

March 1

God's word for today is "eternity."

We as human beings sometimes live our lives as if there is only the present. We are not staying aware that even if we die today, there is a place we will spend "forever" in. What decisions we make now may determine where we spend eternity.

Some people will say, "I do not believe in hell." Whether you believe it or not, the Word of God is true and people are not excluded because they do not believe in it.

God's desire is that none of us perish, but have life eternal with Him. But we have free will and He will not force us to believe.

Some of you know where you are in Christ and I rejoice with you. But if there is someone questioning where their eternal destination is, I urge you to take a moment and confess that Jesus Christ is your Savior.

If you declare with your mouth, "Jesus is Lord," and believe in your heart that God raised him from the dead, you will be saved. For it is with your heart that you believe and are justified, and it is with your mouth that you profess your faith and are saved.
Romans 10:9 (NKJV)

March 2

The concept of Christianity is not a difficult one. Yet many reject the gospel of the Lord Jesus Christ.

The simplicity of salvation can be defined by the first verse in the song "Amazing Grace":

> Amazing grace! (how sweet the sound)
> That saved a wretch like me!
> I once was lost, but now am found,
> Was blind, but now I see.

Jesus is not complicated. Yet His love is beyond all comprehension. A love this deep, this wide, this boundless, cannot be understood within the confines of the human mind. This is one of the reasons many cannot accept Jesus into their hearts. It does not make sense how God came in flesh to give His all for every one of us. It cannot be explained; it must be experienced with the heart.

Those whom He calls His own, He is 100 percent authentic. There are no imitations and no limitations. All who try to duplicate His wonderment will fail miserably.

Although He is pure perfection, He continually gives grace for all our flaws. He is awesome and wonderful! All we need do to be His is to believe and pass on the word. Love never fails!

March 3

Okay, so yesterday felt like a total washout. You lost your temper, road rage reared its ugly head in traffic, yelled at the dog, screamed at the kids. You blew it. Right?

When we attempt to do things in our own strength without enlisting God's help, one thing is sure to happen: failure.

The Bible states, "I can do all things through Christ who strengthens me" (Philippians 4:13 NKJV)

So in our flesh we are not capable of keeping it together. This is why we need Christ every day!

I admittedly try over and over to do things in my own strength. It is just our human nature. But I always fail miserably because I cannot accomplish any good and purposeful thing without God.

The sooner we admit we can do nothing GOOD without Him, the sooner we will have peace, success, love, and happiness within ourselves.

Yes, we are always works in progress. We will never achieve true perfection while here on this earth. But that is what Jesus is for. He holds us together when we fall apart. He soothes us and loves us when we fail miserably. It's His way, it's His grace, it's His love that never fails—even though we always do. But it's okay. His mercies are new every day!

March 4

Guilt is a self-made emotional prison. There is a difference between feeling conviction and feeling condemned.

God convicts when we are doing and saying the wrong things by gently nudging us in the right direction.

The devil condemns us by continuing to plant thoughts in our minds for things we had done in our pasts.

The Bible says, "There is now therefore no condemnation to those who are in Christ Jesus" (Romans 8:1 NKJV).

If we ask for forgiveness He removes our sins as far as the east is from the west and casts them into the sea of forgetfulness (see Psalm 103:12 and Micah 7:19).

Yet many are plagued with guilt from years of mistakes they made.

Have you really given it over to Jesus?

If not, then why not ask Him to take it from you?

He is the burden-bearer and it is His job to handle our guilt and sin.

Just say, "Jesus, please forgive me. Take this burden from me and help me to never take it up again. Help me to take Your yoke upon me, for it is light. Thank You for setting me free!"

So if the Son makes you free, you will be free indeed. John 8:36 (NASB)

March 5

We can rise up in the morning knowing our Master is at
    hand, tirelessly working on our behalf.
No struggling or striving, no worry or care. Jesus Christ is
    on our side. What shall we fear?
Do not be downcast, my friend.
Your valley experience will come to an end.
Just be assured, as sure as you breathe, the Savior is here
    and will bring you relief.
The healing will permeate and saturate through,
Relax and let Jesus do it for you.
He will hold your hand, or cradle your heart,
He knows what your sadness is all about.
Relax, refresh, restore in His grasp,
Let go and let God complete the task.

March 6

Hope is the anchor that casts itself into a sea of faith. Immersing ourselves in prayer and communion with the almighty God is the rock-solid, stabilizing force in an otherwise chaotic world.

He will help you rise above the choppy tumultuous sea of life's circumstances. His love is a lifeboat, a sure footing in the shifting sands. No matter how high the waves, His firm and steady grasp brings us safely to shore. He is our harbor, a refuge in the storm.

As the lighthouse beckons one to safety with its brilliancy, so will the Son bring His beloved home. No mountain is too high, nor pit too deep for Him to find you and rescue you.

Your well-being is ensured as you place your trust in the capable hands of the King of kings.

March 7

Hey, you!

Did you know God thinks you are extraordinary? He created you to be an original, one-of-a-kind masterpiece.

Actually, He is crazy about you! He wants you to know He has great plans for you—plans for a great future. Do not ever doubt God wants you to prosper and to be in health, just as He wants your soul to prosper (see 3 John 2).

How awesome is it that the God of this universe loves you and believes the best for your life? He believes you can do all things through Christ who strengthens you (see Philippians 4:13)!

Now shoot for the stars!

March 8

May I say you are doing a great job!
You wake up and you do this thing called life every day.
It does not matter the mistakes along the way.
It is just like a great big puzzle. Some pieces fit, some do
    not.
What matters is you are trying to do the best you can.
There are times when your best isn't good enough for some
    people.
If you are feeling down on yourself, just remember these
    words:
God loves you, no matter what!
He said to tell you today you are perfectly imperfect
And He is mad about YOU!
You know why?
He loves to busy Himself with every detail of your life.

If you were perfect, that would mean He would be done
    with you.
But He delights in every fracture, every occlusion of your
    earthly being.
And He hums and He smiles as He goes with you about
    your day.
You see, in every way, shape, and form
You are God's masterpiece and He wouldn't have you any
    other way!

March 9

God is rewriting our story—if we let Him!

Oh, the many turns and curves of life indeed! At times it is smooth sailing. But other times it feels as though we are on a long roller coaster that we did not buy a ticket for. The many climbs up the steep slope … the sharp, quick turns … and unknown, sudden dips and drops—they all leave a chronic lump in the throat.

Giving it all over to the Lord, letting Him navigate is the best way to ensure overall peace. He will guard and protect and prevent in all situations. He will strategically redefine our paths—if we give Him the reins.

So give Him over the crumbled pieces of all the yesterdays, where failure was the norm. This is a new day and God will redesign your life and mold it into His work of art!

March 10

You are a one in 7.35 billion.

There is no one else like you. Even if you are an identical twin, your DNA and your fingerprints are like no one else. God's Word says He formed you in your mother's womb, and you are fearfully and wonderfully made (see Psalm 139). No matter how ordinary you feel, God says you are extraordinary!

Not one of us is common. Just as a snowflake magnified is intricate and original, we are also one of a kind. Even more so! We are God's children, and He knows every cell, every gene, in your body. He knows the number of hairs on your head.

Make no mistake: we are God's treasure!

March 11

Many of God's elect in the Bible had to overcome major obstacles to achieve their God-given goals.

David was hunted by King Saul for many years. When given opportunity to kill Saul in his sleep, David refused because he trusted God to bring His plans to fulfillment.

Joseph was sold into slavery by his own brothers and endured many years in prison before his destiny came to fruition.

There are many other examples of people (Ruth, Abraham, Moses, Esther) who stood strong in the face of adversity to hold on to God's promise.

God has a plan for each of us. It is up to us to seek Him and to stay faithful through the "desert seasons" of our lives in order to reach our own promised land.

March 12

Who do you think you are?
I'll tell you who you are not!
You are not the boss of me;
I can see,
What you think you are doing;
Maybe it worked before.
But it's not going to work anymore.
I know your bag of old tricks,
You get your kicks out of pounding me down,
But I've stayed too long on the ground.
So not so fast, you liar,
Set your own pants on fire;
Because I am standing tall,
And even if I fall,
I am bouncing right back up again.
So, fool, don't you pretend,
You have power over me.
I've got the key, you see?
His Name is Jesus,
It's no secret,
He is your kryptonite;
So you can put up a fight,
But you won't win.
He will stand before me again and again.
I am my King's daughter,
And I have a Savior who walks on water.

March 13

God's relationship with us depends solely on our being receptive to Him and spending time in His presence on a regular basis. Because of our free will, God does not chase after His children and force His will on us. He waits for us to extend the invitation and approaches as we invoke His presence. He loves to hear His children talk with Him, and He receives our words with open ears.

The more we connect with God, the closer we feel to Him. As we study His Word, we become more aware of who He is and what He represents. We awaken to the knowledge He is on our side. Therefore, as the Bible says, we can come boldly before His throne to obtain mercy at our time of need (see Hebrews 4:16).

Many do not feel the tangible presence of God, so that makes it difficult to interact with Him as we do with others. As challenging as it may be, we need to practice His presence through conversation and prayer. Continually communicating with God daily will produce a "knowing" of His presence.

Philippians 4:6 states, "Do not fret or have any anxiety about anything, but in every circumstance and in everything, by prayer and petition (definite requests), with thanksgiving, continue to make your wants known to God."

March 14

Break away from the monotony and chaos of the day.

Come sit beside God on Heaven's porch.

We may be limited by our mortality. But by our spirits, we can virtually be transported there.

Take a breath and close your eyes. Be one with the Prince of peace. He is waiting for you now:

"Jesus, I want to feel You close to me now. I yearn to feel Your peace. I have been so busy and I am feeling anxious and uncertain about everything.

Help me to rest and take comfort in Your Words, "Give all your worries and cares to God, for he cares about you."
1 Peter 5:7

Let me make that conscious decision to hand it all over to you, once and for all.

Thank You, Lord for loving me and helping me to let go and let God.

In Your Name I pray. Amen."

March 15

In choosing the path to wholeness, God will desire for us to come to terms with pain from the past and also the present. Sometimes bringing out what is hidden can feel so foreign and unsettling. But the Lord wants us healthy and He desires that we not carry fragments of hate, bitterness, or hurt with us. As God unveils the hurt and pain we buried, our heart may ache with sadness. But as we become more familiarized with His design for healthy resolutions, we discover closure through His peace.

God will teach us balance in being gentle, yet strong in Him and in the power of His might. He will reveal the keys to healthy relations and boundaries with people.

Behold, I am sending you out like sheep in the midst of wolves; be wary and wise as serpents, and be innocent (harmless, guileless, and without falsity) as doves.
Matthew 10:16 (AMPCE)

March 16

Never was there a time where we need Christ more in our lives. The realm between good and evil is being clearly defined. We need Jesus now to help us to stay the course.

He is the beacon of hope in a troubled world. He is our harbor when we need refuge. Though the troubles and concerns can feel overwhelming at times, we can have peace with Christ.

He said:

I'm telling you these things while I'm still living with you. The Friend, the Holy Spirit whom the Father will send at my request, will make everything plain to you. He will remind you of all the things I have told you. I'm leaving you well and whole. That's my parting gift to you. Peace. I don't leave you the way you're used to being left—feeling abandoned, bereft. So don't be upset. Don't be distraught.
John 14:25–27 (THE MESSAGE)

Let us make a choice to draw near to the one who provides the true peace, the *"shalom"* that the world cannot provide. He has power and authority over our state of mind. He stated, "In this world you will have trouble. But take heart! I have overcome the world" (John 16:33 NIV).

March 17

Did someone hurt you, without cause? Has it been years and your heart still stings when you think of what they did to you? Dear friends, I know that feeling.

The most challenging hurt to heal is one that was never validated or resolved. Jesus knew this would be a struggle for us. Many times we will have to take the offense to Him again and again. But He does not want us to feel badly when it is not instantaneously healed.

The deeper the wound, the longer it takes to heal. The Lord knows the struggle is real.

Let's be honest when we tell God, "I am having a problem letting go of this. Help me to forgive."

Some people will just try to bury the offense and forget it. But God would rather have us reveal it to Him and expose it to His love and healing touch. So do not let hurts and pain hide in the shadows. Bring them into the light where God will heal your heart.

March 18

God is love, is health, is happiness, is provision, is salvation, is awesome!

I hear people using the word "awesome" a lot these days.

The dictionary defines awesome as impressive and frightening: so impressive or overwhelming as to inspire a strong feeling of admiration or fear.

To me "awesome" should be reserved for God: "Let them praise your great and awesome name! Holy is he!" (Psalm 99:3 ESV).

He is our wonderful, magnificent, perfect, all-knowing Father! There is nothing too hard for Him: "I am the LORD, the God of all mankind. Is anything too hard for me?" (Jeremiah 32:27 NIV).

At times things may seem like they are never going to work out. But there is a word of hope that resonates in my heart—that He will never leave us or forsake us: "For He [God] Himself has said, I will not in any way fail you nor give you up nor leave you without support. [I will] not, [I will] not, [I will] not in any degree leave you helpless nor forsake nor let [you] down (relax My hold on you)! [Assuredly not!]" (Hebrews 13:5 AMPCE).

WOW! That to me means our Lord will deliver. It may not be when or how we think, but you can rest assured it will be perfect!

That my friend, is AWESOME!

March 19

In the midst of a tender moment,

While I seek having You ever more,

I seize and respond to Your calling,

Your waves billow onto my shore.

I drift in Your water, it soothes me,

I proclaim it is all that I need,

I bask in the wondrous breaking

Of Your healing and tender springs.

The water is ever rising,

But I need not to swim or strive,

I wade in Your marvelous tidings,

I just float and I close my eyes.

But the water that I will give him shall become a spring of water welling up (flowing, bubbling) [continually] within him unto (into, for) eternal life.

John 4:14 (AMPCE)

March 20

What am I doing here? Well, to tell you the truth, sometimes I just don't know. We are being real here, right?

God, show me the way. I want to make a difference on this planet. But I mess up big time. I'm not perfect. But Your incredible love is. I won't linger in feeling unworthy because your grace is sufficient and covers all my sins. I'm flawed but You are not. Thank You, Father, for standing with me in patient compassion.

Sometimes I want to get even when others hurt me. But then You let me know that You love them too and that they deserve grace.

You put up with a lot from us, Lord. But You never give up—no matter what.

And I will keep on keeping on, because You never stop being my God.

March 21

Hey, you over there—in the farthest, smallest corner of the other side of world! I am here to say to you, "God sees you and knows what you're going through!"

It is truly amazing that through the power and ingenuity of social media, we are able to connect with people from all over the world. Yet God, in His infinite power and omnipresence, is connecting with every single one of us all—at the same time!

Let us try to absorb the magnitude of that statement. The Master of the universe, with His awesome abilities and omnipotence, watches me over here while He monitors you over there. Nothing escapes His steady gaze.

You see, "The Lord's arm is not too weak to save you, nor is his ear too deaf to hear you call" (Isaiah 59:1 nlt). No one and nothing is too insignificant for Him to attend to. He cares about every single one of our needs because He cares for us.

He will bring about perfection for our concerns, with the dutiful works of His hands, and cause us to triumph: "The Lord will perfect that which concerneth me: thy mercy, O Lord, endureth forever ..." (Psalm 138:8 kjv), and "Now thanks be unto God, which always causeth us to triumph in Christ, and maketh manifest the savour of his knowledge by us in every place" (2 Cor. 2:14 kjv).

March 22

Hi, it's Jesus. I have lived out My life for this day. I tell you the truth, I knew it was coming. But I wish it would not have come so quickly.

I so enjoyed spending time ministering to the people and teaching My friends how to carry on when I am gone. Last night I prayed for a long time in the garden. Although I knew what was going to happen, part of me longed for another way. But Father said it has to be. Do not be sad, though. I want to do this.

It's not easy. Pain never is. But you are worth it to Me. I want to do everything I can to give you abundant life. Do you not see, you mean everything to me?

Even the ones who do not believe, I love with all my heart. Remember the thieves who hung on My left and right? I love the one who hated Me as much as the one who repented.

My favorite thing to do is to sit beside the Father, praying for you all. You have so much to learn about My love. But I am very patient as I teach you how to walk in compassion.

Do not get angry when others hate you. Remember, they hated me too.

When people are in the dark, the light hurts their eyes. You are the light of the world.

When people are unfair, try to think of my words, "Father, forgive them."

I am right beside you all the time. When life is hard, I'm holding you tight.

I love when you talk to Me. You can tell me anything!

Do not worry about telling Me your thoughts; I know what you are thinking anyhow!

Give Me all of your problems. I love to work them out for you.

My time has come now. But before I go, please remember: Tell others about Me. They need to know that I'm doing this because I love them too.

And whatever you do, never give up on Me. I will never give up on you.

Love,
Jesus

March 23

Cobwebs, dirt, and dust collide,
Welling up in my cavernous mind.
Feelings of hurt, regret, inadequacy,
I thank You, Father, as You are taking me,
Walking me through this journey of healing,
Teaching me to embrace the "me" with real feelings.
You leave no stone unturned, whether heavy or small,
We'll get to the place of true beauty,
You abide through it all.
Oh the mess I left behind for You to clean,
The dark recesses where shadows meet.
And darkness begets darkness,
Oh the dankness of yesteryear streets.
Yet You don't chastise or hurry me,
You glide along, at turtle speed.
You say, "We'll get there, you and I.
I am here right at your side.
I will see you through to see the sun,
Then we will bask in the glory
of the days begun."

March 24

Sometimes it's hard to give—not because you do not want to, but because people think there are always strings attached.

Object of my point: I had an extra hoagie that I decided I would give away. I put it in the refrigerator at work and placed a note on the door that read, "Free hoagie. Please take."

Later that day, I noticed the hoagie was still there. Soon, I overheard the following conversation:

"I don't know. It's still there. I think it's a trap. Who would do that?"

Finally I went out and inquired of the subject of their discussion.

They said, "The hoagie. We think it's a joke."

"Let me solve the mystery," I said with a smile. "I brought it. It's perfectly fine to eat."

It was kind of humorous overhearing them talking about a possible trick hoagie. But it was sad, as many cannot believe we can give without having a motive.

Maybe most are hesitant to accept salvation because they also assume there is a catch. It is totally free—but priceless just the same.

For the wages of sin is death, but the free gift of God is eternal life in Christ Jesus our Lord.
Romans 6:23 (ESV)

March 25

It was the first Palm Sunday. All of Jerusalem came out to greet Jesus, waving and spreading palms on the ground to welcome their Messiah. Their cries: "Hosanna! Blessed is He who comes in the name of the Lord." (See Mark 11:7–10 NASB.)

The high priests and Pharisees scoffed, saying, "This is their king? What king rides on a mule?"

So it began: the plot to discredit Jesus. Their anger raged as Jesus preached words that contradicted everything they believed. Their hatred, burning at a fever pitch, managed to spurn total outrage in the people.

Within days, some of the same people who welcomed the Messiah, yelled, "Crucify Him!"

Yet as he questioned Jesus, Pilate said to Him, "You do not speak to me? Do You not know that I have authority to release You, and I have authority to crucify You?" Jesus answered him, "You would have no authority over Me, unless it had been given you from above." (See John 19:9–11 NASB.)

Jesus knew that when He rode into town, it was the beginning of the end.

Yet He laughed with and loved the people.

Can we fully comprehend the living Son of God, born of flesh, sentenced to death, rejoicing before His execution? No, we cannot. But He did and chose the cross anyway. His love never fails!

March 26

How about that Jesus?
He takes who the world calls foolish,
And makes us into someone who matters.
Life shatters,
But our Savior builds.
We empty, He fills.
I am a former failure,
Until Jesus came my way.
I am feeling free,
I am feeling saved.
He picked me up,
Gave me love.
Helped me see
The good in me.
Oh my Jesus,
How great You are with us.
You love us all the same,
We are all Your favorites,
Even who the world's rejects.
Jesus … there's something about that name!

March 27

Society teaches nothing is free. When you walk into a retail place, you are greeted by a syrupy-sweet employee whose goal is to get your business. Normal, right? But we have been taught by the world's standards that you cannot get something for nothing.

The bottom line: it is extremely hard to trust because we've all been burned before. But God's objective is for us to display His love with no strings attached.

Love is not just a noun; it is a verb. So we need to do more than simply say it; we need to live it.

People will be watching to see if our actions correspond with our words. So be a person committed to loving at all costs, and give it away!

Love is free. But it's priceless just the same!

March 28

I am a human being! Truth be told, I mess up.

I can sure be a whiner. I try to do what's right. But there are times when hell catches my tongue on fire (see James 3:6).

Forget all the ideologies about being a perfect Christian. We know we are going to make mistakes. Do we want to? No.

But when we do, we are forgiven. Christ's gift doesn't give us a license to sin. But it sure feels awesome when we happen to fall short. God knew we would often get ourselves in a pickle.

Jesus gave His all so that we could obtain our "get out of hell free" card. But this isn't a Monopoly game.

It's times like these that we need to appreciate Him the most—when we are least deserving of the gift. With all our unworthiness, He went the distance.

No shortcuts, no sidestepping—it was a clean sweep. He wanted to make sure there were no hidden clauses for our mess-ups.

Yes, it is for real: the love for us.

For God so loved the world that He gave His only begotten son, that whoever believes in Him should not perish but have everlasting life.
John 3:16 (NKJV)

March 29

His eye is on the sparrow and I know He watches me.
Some days we are vulnerable to life's assaults. Whether it
be health, finances, or general discord among us, let us
cling to the truth: the reality of day-to-day unrest is nothing
compared to the ultimate promises God gives.

He is all knowing and aware of the daunting
struggles we face. But He gives us the choice to not face it
alone. The attacks are real. But God is much greater.

Just as the powerful old hymn rings out the truth
that will resound for eternity, He is watchful of all. Every
sparrow, every living being, is within range of His steady
gaze.

How much more are we to our Master than the
sparrow. We are His beloved and He is into every minute
detail of our lives.

Whenever I am tempted, whenever clouds arise,
When songs give place to sighing, when hope within me
dies,
I draw the closer to Him, from care He sets me free;
His eye is on the sparrow, and I know He watches me;
His eye is on the sparrow, and I know He watches me.
—From "His Eye Is on the Sparrow"

by Civilla D. Martin and Charles H. Gabriel

March 30

He is the Prince of Peace,
The Lord of Lords,
The Alpha and Omega,
The Bright and Morning Star.
He is the Beginning and the End.
All that's good and holy
Is in His mighty hands.
He stands at the door and knocks.
His eternal salvation is free,
The preciousness and value
He leaves to you and me.
His Word is a lamp to our feet
And a light to our path.
The joy and peace He gives
Is the one that lasts.
Invite Him into your house this morning,
He is calling out your name,
Open your heart to Jesus,
Life will never, ever be the same.

March 31

I believe that Jesus Christ went down to hell the moment He died. He appeared before the devil. He took the keys to the kingdom of heaven that Satan had held captive for thousands of years.

I believe, Jesus spoiled principalities, thereby freeing our souls and spirits to life eternal.

No longer are we prisoners. For the law of adhering to strict practices to be acceptable to God was eliminated forever by the blood of the Lamb.

He annihilated the works of the flesh by exercising power over evil. As it says in Revelation 1:18 (KJV), "I am he that liveth, and was dead; and, behold, I am alive for evermore, Amen; and have the keys of hell and of death."

But to each one of us grace has been given as Christ apportioned it. This is why it says: "When he ascended on high, he took many captives and gave gifts to his people." (What does "he ascended" mean except that he also descended to the lower, earthly regions? He who descended is the very one who ascended higher than all the heavens, in order to fill the whole universe.) So Christ himself gave the apostles, the prophets, the evangelists, the pastors and teachers, to equip his people for works of service, so that the body of Christ may be built up until we all reach unity in the faith and in the knowledge of the Son of God and become mature, attaining to the whole measure of the fullness of Christ.
Ephesians 4:7–10 (NIV)

April 1

Now a word from our Sponsor:

Hello, My sweet child. I see you are struggling in this life. Do not panic. I am here to comfort you. I will give you rest from your anxiety and fear. I ask you to just stop for a moment and come near to Me. Seek My face, and the concerns of this life will dim and fade in the presence of My love.

I want you to have peace. But you toil and spin so. Let Me in and I will give you comfort. Just rely on My ability to transform your countenance.

I am the Lord who changes not and I will always be here for you. I love you.

Just come to Me and I will hold you in My arms until the storm passes.

April 2

Some days are just great.
Everything falls into place.
Then there are times I can't stand,
I'm flying by the seat of my pants.
I just want some relief,
God, give me some time to breathe.
I love I can be real with You,
Lord,
I'm counting on better days for Your girl.
I will praise You through the exhaustion,
And sing to You when I feel like yelling.
Okay, I'll stop complaining,
I know You are teaching me patience.
I will aim to keep on stepping
To the rhythm of Your heart's inflection.
I will trust in You no matter what,
You will bring me through,
You are my God.

April 3

She stood in the checkout line, with a young girl at her side. They each had a large bag of potatoes in hand. The woman then asked the cashier to weigh the potatoes to see which one was heavier, to get a better value.

The woman had two dollars in hand and the girl pulled out an ACCESS Card.

The girl said to the clerk, "There should be two dollars on the card."

That was about the time I heard God say, "Pay for their potatoes."

As I did so, the girl and the woman said in unison, "Thank you!"

I do not say this to receive a pat on the back or praise. I am telling you that, not so long ago, I was the one in line, buying potatoes. At the time, potatoes were all I could afford. I promised the Lord, when the day came, I would pay it forward.

We are so blessed to be able to go pick up groceries when we need them. So I ask you, on your trips to the market, to keep your eyes open for the ones in need. Do not be afraid to embarrass, or cause a scene. God will give you a perfect opportunity to be a blessing.

Going back to the story, just as I turned the corner in my car, I saw them walking ahead of me. I rolled down the window and gave them five dollars.

"Thank you so much," the lady said with tears in her eyes.

Never forget your potato days.

April 4

"I have felt the sting of darkness and death until it drew me to my knees, begging for God to release me, or take me home." Oftentimes, these words are the very familiar plea that echo through the chambers of many hearts. At times we question why after many years, we still experience the days that David so accurately described in Psalm 13 (NIV):

> How long, LORD? Will you forget me forever?
> How long will you hide your face from me?
> How long must I wrestle with my thoughts?
> And day after day have sorrow in my heart?
> Give light to my eyes, or I will sleep in death,
> and my enemy will say, "I have overcome him,"
> and my foes will rejoice when I fall.
> But I trust in your unfailing love;
> my heart rejoices in your salvation.
> I will sing the LORD's praise,
> for he has been good to me.

No matter who or what our battle's with, we can forge on knowing God will utilize the heartache for His purposes.

David went on to be the anointed king of Israel. Often a great burden precedes a great blessing. God can use the very same brutal experience that wracked your mind and body, to serve as a comfort to others in need.

He is a God who never wastes anything. Our pain will be someone's gain, and He is the reason we can smile through the rain.

April 5

Persevere through the fire. Do the right thing, even when the wrong thing is happening. Stand through the trials until the victory is won.

Jesus already obtained the victor's crown and He is waiting for us at the finish line, cheering us on! I can hear Him shouting, "I believe in you. You can do it! Just believe in Me!"

Believe in the words that "He is a rewarder of those who diligently seek Him" (Hebrews 11:6 NKJV). Forget all the negative voices you have heard all your life. Blessed assurance is having faith in the Rock of our salvation. He is the key to success in overcoming adversity.

You are in it to win it. Go and grow!

April 6

*And be constantly renewed in the spirit of your mind...,
and put on the new nature ... created in God's image, ... in
true righteousness and holiness.*
Ephesians 4:23–24 (AMPCE)

Being renewed in your mind means to continually cast
down every thought that exalts itself against the true
knowledge of God's Word (2 Corinthians 10:5).

Our minds are carnal and are subject to human
thoughts (Romans 8:6). Without the Holy Spirit to aid us
every day, we are weak against the attacks of the enemy
(Romans 8:26–27).

When we enlist the help of the Holy Spirit, we
exchange our weaknesses for God's strength, our words for
God's Word, our wickedness for God's love.

With God's Spirit inside of us, He will make us
aware of a potentially sinful situation before it happens.
You may have an angry thought and want to speak angry
words. The Bible tells us, "In your anger, do not
sin."(Ephesians 4:26 NIV) It does not say not to feel anger.
The Bible says, "I will take heed and guard my ways, that I
may sin not with my tongue; I will muzzle my mouth as
with a bridle while the wicked are before me" (Psalm 39:1
AMPCE).

Anger is a human emotion. Jesus felt anger, but He
did not allow His anger to cause Him to sin. He relied on
the Holy Spirit to help Him choose words that reflected
God's love.

April 7

He who knew no sin, became sin for you and me (2 Corinthians 5:21). Every sin we ever committed, and ever will commit, is covered by the blood of Jesus.

He came and remained a spotless Lamb, without blemish or sin. His sole purpose: a divine sacrifice, set apart by God to be the pardon for our countless infractions against each other and ultimately against God. It is because of Jesus that God will say, "I will remember your sins no more" (see Isaiah 43:25 and Hebrews 8:12).

If you feel like you are under condemnation and you think to yourself, *God will never forgive what I did,* then you are saying the sacrifice of Jesus Christ was not enough and was inferior in some way. We all know that nothing could be further from the truth.

As He hung on that cross, His last Words were, "It is finished." His merciful sacrifice once and for all abolished hell's power over us. We have been freed from the clutches of evil forever, if we make the right choice.

April 8

We've seen worse times and we have also seen better. Sometimes we feel like we are drowning. I know we will get through this. God, you got this, right?

Then we hear a voice that says, "Don't struggle and strive. Just lie on your back and float, as I carry your cares away with the waves."

Soon, as we let our cares take over again, we begin to sink. But Jesus reaches down and pulls us from the depths of despair and sets us on a solid rock.

We are safe and sound. We're rescued once again.

He is our Jesus. He is our "Life Savior."

April 9

I am grateful beyond words,

For the opportunity God affords.

He shines His love down for free,

How very blessed are you and me.

I thank You, Lord, from the bottom of my heart,

To show my gratitude, where do I start?

I'm going to spread the word,

Hey you there! Have you heard?

About the awesome abundant love,

From a Lord who is crazy about us.

He will take you from the darkest place,

Shine His light upon your face.

Cleanse you from the sin and pain,

He's the super washer of our human stain.

Beauty from ashes, that is His part,

Wonderful Jesus, the mender of hearts!

April 10

He is crazy about you, you know!

Forget all the self-imposed guilt and track record of screw-ups. He doesn't want your guilt. He wants your love.

It's daunting to conceive that the Lord of all the universe forgives and forgets our sins. The Bible says He tosses our sins into the sea of forgetfulness (Micah 7:19).

All we need do is repent. Repenting means to turn away from. Repenting and forgiveness is a byproduct of being in Christ.

He forgives because He loves and will always love, no matter what. The debt for our worst sins has been cancelled. You don't have to work to pay it back, or earn His favor. You are already the King's chosen. This everlasting love means *forever*. We are all His favorite child.

When I think of how long it has taken me to grasp this ... Good gravy!

But it's in the vault and nothing's taking it out! So I am spreading the news to you:

Extra, extra read all about it!

God is so in love with you!

April 11

He is the burden-bearer. He is the repairer of the breech; the restorer of streets to dwell on.

All that is good and holy comes from Him. He will restore all the years that evil has stolen from you.

Do not be afraid to give it all over to Him. The nail-scarred hands are big enough to hold every drop of your precious tears.

He waits to carry the load of your troubles.

He wants to give you life everlasting.

He wants to know you.

Introduce yourself. Jesus is dying to talk with you!

April 12

*Now I beseech you, brethren, by the name of our Lord
Jesus Christ, that ye all speak the same thing, and that
there be no divisions among you; but that ye be perfectly
joined together in the same mind and in the same judgment.
For it hath been declared unto me of you, that there are
contentions among you. Now this I say, that every one of
you saith, I am of Paul; and I of Apollos; and I of Cephas;
and I of Christ. Is Christ divided? was Paul crucified for
you? or were ye baptized in the name of Paul?*
1 Corinthians 1:10–13 (KJV)

Jesus believed in love, the new commandment. The
Pharisees abhorred His resistance to religion and it drove
them to put Him to death.
Let us remember to not look at what makes us different.,
but instead to focus on what Jesus talked about: love.

Love transcends all denominations, believes the
best of each other, and above all, Love never fails.

Everyone needs Jesus. They may not know they
need Him. But they need Him just the same.

We are here to be the hands and feet and
mouthpiece of our Lord. If you have someone on your heart
and an opportunity arises, offer a message of life about
Jesus. It may be their last chance to get out of hell.

April 13

Let us rejoice in our God when our feet hit the floor in the morning. May we have an attitude of gratitude. Forgive us, Lord, for those "Why me?" days when we wallow in sorrow.

Help lift us when we are sinking low. For we will yet praise You, our Savior in the land of the living. We will boast in Your goodness and love. You have done wonderful things for us and our souls know it well.

You are our rock to stand on when the waters grow deep. You are our balm to soothe us from the pain and hurt of life.

May we sear Your mercy, love, and truth upon our hearts and cling to Your Word.

Jesus, our breath of life, there is no one like You.

April 14

We all have opportunities to feel negative about life. Past failures and continual setbacks will cause us to feel disheartened from time to time.

When I start to feel discouraged, I decide to have a grateful and thankful heart for everything I do have.

I was very low on gas one morning and I needed what I had to last me until the following day. Instead of worrying, I decided to thank the Lord for His many provisions.

The Bible says, "My God shall supply all your need according to His riches in glory by Christ Jesus" (Philippians 4:19 NKJV). That is not according to our bank statement, or what is in our wallets. God's word says He owns "Cattle on a thousand hills." There is nothing He cannot help us with. So may we always pray:

Dear God,

Thank you for all Your wondrous gifts!

Help us to adopt an attitude of gratitude and always be thankful for our blessings.

We will continue to rest in the knowledge you know all of our needs. We trust you to provide what is good and beneficial for us.

In Jesus's name, amen.

April 15

Adoration and exultation were the sentiments of the crowd as the Lord Jesus entered into town. With palms waving and being laid before his feet, they welcomed the Messiah.

Soon, very soon, though, the tables would turn. The same ones who welcomed him later scorned Him, cursed Him, calling for His death. How very crushed Jesus must have felt.

The populace raged against the Prince of Peace.

They hated Him. But Jesus knew what was behind the shroud of scorn. The enemy of His and our souls wanted Jesus to break, to give in, and to quit. The flames of hell intensified. But our savior, hero, and friend never wavered. He bore it all for us all.

Today we stand redeemed, forgiven, and accepted by God.

What a day it was when God's love was brought into completion.

April 16

Have you ever seen that old Ajax cleaner commercial with the slogan "Stronger than Dirt!"? God is so clever, and at times humorous, as He brings these nostalgic things to my remembrance to illustrate a life lesson. So let's begin:

I speak to you, as He speaks to me,
At times in poetic form, as you see,
That if we are to be of service,
To make our lives have real purpose,
We must be "Stronger than Dirt,"
To rise above the hate, the hurt;
All the muck, and all the mire,
The consequences are most dire.
I speak to you, as I preach to myself,
Sometimes this life can just be hell.
God says, "Hey, My child, don't throw in the towel!"
(Speaking in all capital letters now)
Devil, you'd sure like us to take a bow.
But we're all in this together,
We will not get hurt,
Cause we are "Stronger than Dirt!"

Faithful is He Who is calling you [to Himself] and utterly trustworthy, and He will also do it [fulfill His call by hallowing and keeping you].
                    1 Thessalonians5:24(AMPCE)

April 17

The very same God who brought you out of captivity is the very same one who will bring you forth to serve Him.

He is the God of Abraham, Isaac, and Jacob. There are no other gods before Him.

With Jacob's son Joseph, God used a prison sentence to give Joseph a passion and purpose to save the lost. A kingdom was won over because of one man.

Moses, a man who stuttered and stammered, brought God's people into the Promised Land.

David, even though he sinned against the Father, was called a man after God's own heart.

Paul seemed born and bred to hate the Christians. Yet the Lord arrested his heart on the road to Damascus, and he became Jesus's greatest warrior of his time.

I am talking about radical conversion!

The pain that you've been feeling can't compare to the joy that is coming!

Saddle up for the greatest adventure of your life!

April 18

Great things are created in the fire of affliction! The heat intensifies, and the substance that was once solid succumbs to the intensity of the temperature. The fire is relentless until all the impurities are burned up. It is 100 percent pure and ready to mold into any shape.

Beautiful creations of gold can only be made because the precious metal goes through the fire. Likewise God uses our struggles to burn and trim off what is not good, to create a vessel worthy to be used for His purpose. So let us hold fast in God's ability to remain faithful and carry us through every trial.

Now to Him who is able to do exceedingly abundantly above all that we ask or think, according to the power that works in us.
Ephesians 3:20 (NKJV)

April 19

Without God we would know no real love. The most famous Bible verse says, "For God so loved the world that He *gave* His only begotten Son, that whoever believes in Him should not perish but have everlasting life" (John 3:16 NKJV, my emphasis added).

It is difficult to understand that kind of love. Each one of us is loved with the intensity of life and death.

Bottom line: Jesus was born to die, so we could love, live, and have the ultimate promise of a home in heaven.

Our objective, as a child of God, is to spread His love to all who need it, regardless if we think they are deserving or not.

Jesus is relentless in His goal of enlisting candidates for His cause. Spread the word to other: "Jesus is dying to meet you!"

April 20

But we have this treasure in earthen vessels, that the excellency of the power may be of God, and not of us.
2 Corinthians 4:7 (KJV)

The treasure is not buried deep in the ground, nor at the bottom of the sea. It is priceless. Yet it is free. It lives on the inside of us all. To access and utilize it, we may endure persecution and pain by the opposing forces.

The treasure many times expires and is wasted, as the recipient's body lies still, forever silenced in the grave.

If I am to speak one thing, let me implore you to not waste your treasure. For you cannot measure in silver or gold, the God-given gift of Jesus Christ you now hold.

April 21

When all else fails, God is faithful! Whatever the world throws your way, know that God is always on your side. He will never leave you nor forsake you. He will never abandon you. He will never leave you as an orphan. How do I know? He says it in His Word!

It is hard to trust when the ones we consider the closest to us have hurt us. Sometimes we protect ourselves by putting up a wall. God's Word instructs us to guard our hearts with "all diligence" (Proverbs 4:23 NKJV). But sometimes in the process we close our hearts and even God cannot get in.

At those times I enlist God's help by simply asking Him to help me to be open to Him. King David, who was a man after God's own heart, asked God to aid him in this battle: "Create in me a clean heart, O God, and renew a right, persevering, and steadfast spirit in me" (Psalm 51:10 AMPCE).

A clean heart is a vessel that is not filled with hatred, bitterness, pity, sorrow, anger, envy, and the like. Remember, although we may be able to conceal our feelings from everyone else, we cannot hide anything from God. He is the One who truly knows it all!

Let us all allow Him to do a "clean sweep" of our hearts daily by asking Him to do so.

April 22

Life's troubles are fleeting,
So I say, keep believing.
What was yesterday disappears,
Hand it all to the One who cares.
He will take your tomorrows,
Life and all its sorrows,
He'll exchange beauty for ashes for you,
Miracles are what our God will do.
He can transform any tragedy,
No matter the severity,
Into love and great beauty.
So don't give up on your dreams.
Take it from me,
He is the authority
And He will restore your peace.
Just give Him the pieces
Of a life, tattered and torn.
He'll rebuild broken, shattered
Hopes,
A life care worn.
You will see my friend,
What our Lord can do,
Lay it all down at the cross,
Let Him change your life for you.

April 23

Blessed is she who has believed that the Lord would fulfill
his promises to her!
Luke 1:45 (NIV)
These were the words that Mary's cousin, Elizabeth, said to
her, as Mary entered her house, carrying the Messiah.

We all can learn a lot from Mary. The cards were
stacked against her. Having a baby out of wedlock was a
formula for being shunned and even stoned. Holding on to
the promise of God through the voice of the angel couldn't
have been easy. But nothing worthwhile ever is.

No matter what came her way, she held on to her
rock and fortress, her Lord.

And Mary said:
"My soul glorifies the Lord
and my spirit rejoices in God my Savior,
for he has been mindful
of the humble state of his servant.
From now on all generations will call me blessed,
for the Mighty One has done great things for me—
holy is his name.
His mercy extends to those who fear him,
from generation to generation.
He has performed mighty deeds with his arm;
He has helped his servant Israel,
remembering to be merciful
to Abraham and his descendants forever, just as he
promised our ancestors."
Luke 1:46–55 (NIV)

April 24

.

The question for us today is not "Could you?" but "Would you?" I heard it said that God does not call the equipped, but He equips the called!

One day I was driving in my car, and I felt the Lord put upon my heart to go see a certain person and pray for her. At that time I felt very insecure and quite inept to pray out loud with someone.

I said, "Lord, I do not think I can do that!"

Immediately I felt the Lord answer back, "I didn't ask you if you *could*. I asked you if you *would*!"

You see, I think sometimes we miss the point. When we are challenged to do something for the kingdom of God, we naturally look at our flaws and shortcomings. But when we do that, we take God out of the equation.

He spoke to my heart one time: "When you are willing, I will make you able!"

In the Bible, God used Moses to do great exploits. Yet, looking at the scriptures, we can see that Moses had some issues: "Then Moses said to the LORD, 'Please, Lord, I have never been eloquent, neither recently nor in time past, nor since You have spoken to Your servant; for I am slow of speech and slow of tongue" (Exodus 4:10 NASB).

Moses may have stuttered, or had a lisp. We really do not know for sure. But we know God used him mightily to save a nation.

Never put limits on how God can use you.

April 25

Even when I am uncertain, God is sure!

Thank You, Lord, that You do not judge us on the basis of our emotions.

God is steadfast and unwavering. His love, provision, and protection is not based upon how we feel. Although in times of uncertainty, we may feel we are on shaky ground, God is 100 percent solid and He never relaxes His hold on us.

Emotions, although real, are not to be trusted. Reliance upon God's Word, instead of feelings, will never disappoint.

I once heard it said, "I won't be moved by how I feel. I hold fast to the Word of God that's real."

He turns our mourning into dancing. He gives us beauty for ashes. Surely only goodness and mercy will follow us all the days of our lives. We will dwell in the house of the Lord forever.

April 26

Unless the LORD builds the house, the builders labor in vain. Unless the LORD watches over the city, the guards stand watch in vain.
Psalm 127:1 (NIV)

Let us rely upon the power and grace of God, not of our works to achieve in life. Many people toil endlessly, without the feeling of satisfaction for their labors. It is sad that their minds will not let them rest.

It is the peace of God, which passes all understanding, that will help us achieve freedom from toiling.

Many people will worry themselves sick. I know I have spent many days worrying about things I have no control over. That's why I am proactive about giving things over to the Lord, who is much more capable of handling my cares than me.

Give it all over to the Lord and rest your weary mind. Remember, God is up all night anyway.

April 27

Be a light in a dark place!
If things look dark and grim,
be the one who brings the light into the room.
Jesus said we are the light of the world.
We must let our light shine before men, so they may see
our Jesus is the way!
The difference is we carry the Son of God in us.
When the Son shines through us, His goodness radiates and
all will know we are unique.
Some days I do not feel like "shining."
I feel misery and I want to wallow in it.
But that does not mean I will continue to go down that
path.
Purposeful positivity is better than anger by accident.
I will continue to look at the silver lining in the dark cloud.
Even though I am not perfect, I serve a Savior who loves
me just the same.
Now that is something to smile about!

*You are the light of the world. A town built on a hill cannot
be hidden. Neither do people light a lamp and put it under
a bowl. Instead they put it on its stand, and it gives light to
everyone in the house. In the same way, let your light shine
before others, that they may see your good deeds and
glorify your Father in heaven.*
Matthew 5:14–16 (NIV)

April 28

To rejoice is a choice! Sometimes I feel like a hypocrite because I still struggle with the things I share with others on social media. Yet God reminds me that I am a work in progress. I am on the Potter's wheel.

I have bad days like all of you. But I know what I am supposed to do when I feel down in the dumps: rejoice! The Bible says we can put on the garment of praise and let go of the spirit of heaviness (see Isaiah 61:3). When we praise and give glory to God, darkness flees!

The devil tries every day to give us something to be upset, sad, and angry about. When we rejoice, God provides the weapons to stave off all the artillery the annoying one can dish out. So sing a song unto the Lord when darkness comes to knock at your door!

In Philippians 4:11–13 (NASB), Paul said:

Not that I speak from want, for I have learned to be content in whatever circumstances I am. I know how to get along with humble means, and I also know how to live in prosperity; in any and every circumstance I have learned the secret of being filled and going hungry, both of having abundance and suffering need. I can do all things through Him who strengthens me.

April 29

I know it sounds crazy,

But the thought just occurred to me:

I would much rather be

A bubble than a rock.

As I was washing my face,

Bubbles appeared.

Pretty to look at, lighter than air.

A rock is a rock; it is always the same.

What would it be like to never change?

Bubbles are see-through,

They reflect the light,

They don't last forever,

But they bring us delight.

In a world where the dark and the strange take space,

Lord, don't let me get stuck in a rocky place.

Let me be pleasant, light, and airy,

Honest, transparent, and especially caring.

Bubbles can float and fly in the air,

Rocks, they just kind of sit there.

I do not want to sink like a rock, in distress,

My desire is to rise far above the mess.

God, help me to not be weighed down with troubles,

Let me be carefree and light like a bubble.

April 30

The dream lives inside you. Don't settle for ordinary. You were born for greatness. Now, live big! Ask God for guidance and give it your all. It does not matter who applauds you. Just kindle the flame with your faith and nothing will stop you.

Setbacks and falls will occur. But don't be afraid to come back home to Him, and He'll give you flying lessons.

Extraordinary doesn't happen overnight. Whatever the vision is, take a chance.

Don't just do life killing time. Embrace it with passion.

And do not waste a single moment saying "I can't." Just believe!

May 1

"Leave it to God to make something out of nothing!" These were the last words I said in a dream one night.

I was speaking these words to a friend. I began to testify of God's ability to make a "nothing" like me, into a "someone" He can use to advance the gospel of Jesus Christ.

You see, many days I still feel like a nobody. But I know that is a lie.

In Christ, we can do all things.

The notion that we are zeros is one of smoke and mirrors, sent from the kingdom of hell to distract us from His mission for my life.

If God's Word tells me I can say, "I am the righteousness of God through Christ," then it is the truth and let's stick with it! (See 2 Corinthians 5:21.)

It does not matter how we feel. Our life relies on the Word of God.

On His Word, we will stand. All other ground is sinking sand.

May 2

God is into the details!

Do we sometimes underestimate God? I know I do. When there is something I am thinking about that I consider insignificant, I find myself thinking, *God is too busy to be bothered with this.*

This comes from our limited flesh mind-set. When we consider God, we have to think out of the box. That takes faith!

I began utilizing God's assistance by asking Him to help me find things that are missing. If I am searching for something, I will say, "Lord, help me find the object that I am looking for."

If I am looking for a parking place, I will ask God to help me find one. He always gets me the perfect spot!

God's Word says that He will perfect that which concerns us, meaning He will make right what is wrong with us (see Psalm 138:8).

I love that we can come right to our Abba Daddy and tell Him exactly what is wrong.

I love that He loves us sooo much that He will never say, "Go away! Can't you see I'm busy?"

Never, ever believe the lie that He does not care how you feel. He loves us all with an everlasting and agape (unconditional) love. That means no matter what, no matter how, He always loves. It's just who He is.

He is love!

May 3

Don't stop believing! You got this. You're in the home stretch. You may be tired. Your muscles might be aching from the race. But whatever you do, do not give up!

God has your answer, your breakthrough after the hurdle. He knows you are weary. Ask Him and He will infuse you with the strength to go another mile. Thank Him for getting you this far. I know it's hard. But stand in faith. You have gone too far to turn back now.

Proceed in the knowledge that God has got your back, and that He will not quit on you. Keep moving forward—crawl if you must. But just go! Your miracle is waiting!

May 4

Words for today (and every day): Never, ever, ever GIVE UP!

God is going to do something special for you, through you, and in you. Sometimes we think it is never going to happen. We have prayed for years and things have not changed. Yet we do not see what God is doing behind the scenes.

You see my friends, our continual prayers are the breeding ground for a miracle! As it says in James 5:16 (AMPCE), "The earnest (heartfelt, continued) prayer of a righteous man makes tremendous power available [dynamic in its working]."

We have been depressed, we have been in despair, but we must never give up prayer. It is our direct connection with our Lord. He listens and regards our prayers. He knows our needs, but as we continually pray, He sees our faith and as He is working in our situation, lining up every single area. He is saying, "Here is My peace, My child. Keep the line of communication open so I may transform you during the times you are waiting for the promise!"

Our God is always on the job! Here are the words of Jesus:

Then He spoke a parable to them, that men always ought to pray and not lose heart.

Luke 18:1 (NKJV)

May 5

In the quest to reach our desires and goals in life, do we sometimes leave God behind? Many times I believed I knew better than God in realizing my dreams, desires, etc., and I decided to forge out on my own. In spite of the still, small voice inside echoing the gentle words, "Do not go there," I stayed my own course.

Oh, the regrets we feel when we do not submit to the voice of God. I have learned and I am still learning that God does not want His children to be unhappy, lacking, and feel unfulfilled. He only desires to give us His very best.

When we are on the wrong path, we cannot expect His blessings on our lives. Sometimes it is difficult to wait for what God has for us. But if we do, He promises the reward is definitely worth the wait.

Days will come where we steer off course. But with God's grace, we can get back on track and start again. God is full of new beginnings!

Let us not become weary in doing good, for at the proper time we will reap a harvest if we do not give up.
Galatians 6:9 (NKJV)

May 6

My Jesus,
Stand in the gap for me,
I did not see
How these hurts
Could cut so deep.
I was blinded,
Now I grieve.
My heart needs mending,
Your touch will renew,
It sends tender healing,
Your love, how it soothes.
Jesus, be my lover,
My friend, in need,
Breathe on me Your blessed love,
Refresh this weary being.

May 7

Jesus tells us in His Word, "In this world you will have trouble. But take heart! I have overcome the world." John 16:33 NIV

This world, with its chaos, brings misery, depression, sin, and hate into our lives. We must learn to go to the cross with all the issues we carry. We can lay them down at Jesus's feet and rest in the knowledge that He will take care of it all.

I am a witness to the fact God will never let us down. Deuteronomy 31:8 states, "The LORD himself goes before you and will be with you; he will never leave you nor forsake you. Do not be afraid; do not be discouraged."

Many people, including our kin, may have hurt us. But God will never relax His hold on us. He is forever faithful!

May 8

*Come to Me, all you who labor and are heavy laden, and I
will give you rest. Take My yoke upon you and learn from
Me, for I am gentle and lowly in heart, and you will find
rest for your souls. For My yoke is easy and My burden is
light.*
Matthew 11:28–30 (NKJV)

The first four letters in the word *restoration* are R-E-S-T.
Yes, with God's blessing comes resting—resting in His
love, His peace, His Word. Resting does not mean
worrying, fretting, or being anxious about issues we have
no control over. God's Word states: "Casting the whole of
your care [all your anxieties, all your worries, all your
concerns, once and for all] on Him, for He cares for you
affectionately and cares about you watchfully" (1 Peter 5:7
AMPCE).

Therefore, we must make a conscience decision to
cast all our cares upon God. In the secret, quiet place, the
distracting elements of our lives are stilled by the serenity
of being one with God. In that time, He speaks softly the
ministering words of love to His precious children. He
knows exactly our needs. He is aware of our hearts. He sees
our beginning from our end.

A small glimpse into His goodness will cast radiant
light on any situation, no matter how dark it appears.

In the quiet places, we can create one solitary
setting in the midst of our being, where no one else can
go—just us and God.

May 9

While looking through some memorabilia recently, I came upon a picture of Christ. This depiction of Jesus represents many things to me. When I was a young girl (eighteen to twenty years old), I endured one of the most excruciating seasons of my life. Anxiety, depression, and great fear overtook me. I suffered mainly in silence.

At night I trembled from head to toe in terror, believing I was losing my sanity. How wicked the enemy is to prey upon someone young and impressionable.

I would sleep with this very picture of Christ in my grasp, night after night. I knew the Lord was there. But somehow I felt unworthy, excluded from His grace. This picture *The Sacred Heart of Jesus* somehow kept me together when everything was falling apart.

Oh how I wish I knew then, what I know now.

His grace, His love, His power is sufficient and readily available no matter how lowly we feel. We are all living proof.

May 10

The road to Calvary was littered with our sins, fears, diseases, our scars of life. The debt was paid. He paid for everything, once and for all. No longer do we have to wonder if our sins are forgiven. If we ask for forgiveness, Jesus will wipe the slate clean.

The wonderful, awesome work of the cross!

We were once dead. As a new creation in Christ, we are restored as new. We are born again—alive in Christ.

You may have heard this message many times. But we need to appreciate the magnitude of the message!

Jesus suffered, died, and rose from the dead so we can be forever free. The cross is a constant reminder we will never be a slave to sin again! Heaven is our home!

Grace be to you and peace from God the Father, and from our Lord Jesus Christ, who gave himself for our sins, that he might deliver us from this present evil world, according to the will of God and our Father: to whom be glory for ever and ever. Amen.

Galatians 1:3–5 (KJV)

May 11

And being in agony He was praying very fervently; and His
sweat became like drops of blood, falling down upon the
ground.
Luke 22:44 (NASB)

While in the Garden of Gethsemane, Jesus suffered such
extreme emotional anguish that the Bible says, "His sweat
became like drops of blood." Some may dismiss this verse
as figurative and not literal.

Science also has a valid explanation for what
happened to Jesus that night: "Hematidrosis" is a rare, but
very real, medical condition in which one's sweat will
contain blood. The sweat glands are surrounded by blood
vessels. At times of extreme stress, these vessels can
constrict and then dilate to the point of rupture, thereby
causing the blood to effuse into the sweat glands.

We can see the anguish of Jesus that night in
Matthew 26:36 (NIV): "My soul is overwhelmed with
sorrow to the point of death."

We remember Jesus's death when we read this
account in the Bible—or when we see it portrayed before
our eyes. As I sat in the theater watching Christ's
crucifixion, I hid my eyes. I heard in my spirit that moment,
"If you cannot witness My suffering, you cannot take part
in My joy."

And so, in spite of how much we hate what
atrocities Christ suffered, we must also remember the great
sacrifice was all for us. He gave it all for love!

May 12

Say to yourself: "This is the beginning of a new day. I am embracing my fresh start. If God be for me, who can be against me? Greater is He who is in me, than he that is in the world."

We may have had a rough beginning, but we have overcome many obstacles. Instead of focusing on our past failures, let us take a moment to recognize our triumphs.

Being overcomers means we have the tenacity to do wonderful things, despite our mistakes. Now we can say to ourselves, "I had a bad day yesterday. But with Christ, I am anticipating a victorious day!"

We are standing at the summit of the mountain and proclaiming we are triumphant! Let us seek God in everything we do and He will maximize our potential for greatness.

Yet in all these things we are more than conquerors
through Him who loved us.
Romans 8:37 (NKJV)

May 13

The tale of Ruth is a true biblical account of a woman's struggle to persevere through extreme hardship and staying true to God and family.

There was a great famine in the land. Ruth had lost her husband. Naomi, Ruth's mother-in-law, had lost her own husband and her two sons. Naomi had no other choice but to return to her home town of Bethlehem.

She bid her daughters-in law farewell. But Ruth refused to let Naomi leave without her.

Ruth was born a Moabite, and Naomi, a Jew. Something drew Ruth to leave her home region, her family, and her familiar surroundings behind. That something was God.

Following Christ usually means stepping out into uncharted territories. But the rewards are quite worthwhile as we trust in God for a plan for our lives.

But Ruth said, "Do not urge me to leave you or turn back from following you; for where you go, I will go, and where you lodge, I will lodge. Your people shall be my people, and your God, my God. Where you die, I will die, and there I will be buried. Thus may the LORD do to me, and worse, if anything but death parts you and me."

Ruth 1:15–16 (NASB)

May 14

God's track record for coming through is 100 percent! I am thinking on all those times of desperation, where I didn't know how I was going to make it. But guess what? I made it!

It was in those hard times, I learned to rely on God because I had nothing else. It was a time God used to build my faith and to really trust Him.

Sure, it is tough when we are going through the valley. But He will always walk us through, if we allow Him.

I realized the times when I took to worrying, I was taking my eyes off of God. Many tears and tense times later, I now know He is in control of my concerns, my well-being, my destiny.

Leave it to the Lord to handle your life. He will make sure everything will turn out right.

Dear Lord,

I am concerned about a lot of things. Today I make a choice to give it all to You. I believe You will handle all my problems because You love me and want the very best for me. Thank You for helping me and giving me peace. In Jesus's name, amen.

May 15

If at first you don't succeed, you are human!

You have blown your diet after the umpteenth try, and you feel like a failure. Your intentions were misunderstood by a friend, and they are hurt. Your boss passed over you once again for the promotion. You had a fender bender just after you had your car fixed. These and more are scenarios that have the potential to wreak havoc in our life—if we allow them to.

Many times I have succumbed to a bad day, as I've felt weakened by the adversity. Because we all experience misfortune in life, we need to be aware that there is an enemy at large. His vocation is to steal, kill, and destroy. As children of God, we are always on the chopping block. Every day the enemy is using people, situations, and things as bait to steal our joy. The key to overcoming hinges in the words, "The joy of the LORD is your strength" (Nehemiah 8:10 NIV).

May 16

The same God that saved Noah from the flood and the same that parted the sea for Moses, is the same God who will save us from our circumstances.

Yea, though we walk through the valley, He is with us! He will never leave us or forsake us. Hold on to the promises of God like a dog with a bone.

Place all your cares in the Master's hands. Do not take them back. Let Him transform your messes into a message, your trials into triumph. He loves us as if we are His only child.

His love will heal the broken pieces of our heart and restore all our shattered yesterdays. We are blessed, favored, and loved.

May 17

He will give us beauty for ashes (see Isaiah 61:3), and He will turn our mourning into dancing (see Psalm 30:11). And as is says in Psalm 23: "Yea, though I walk through the valley of the shadow of death … thou art with me; thy rod and thy staff they comfort me…. Surely goodness and mercy shall follow me all the days of my life: and I will dwell in the house of the LORD forever" (vv. 4, 6 KJV). These are wonderful words of God that hold promises for us all!

Everyone experiences trials in life. God is the key to sustaining us through the valleys. The low points we face might be sickness, poverty, unhappiness, anger, mourning the death of a loved one, or many other things. Whatever it might be, the Word assures us He will supply our every need according to His riches in Christ Jesus (see Philippians 4:19).

God has an abundance of supply. The Bible says that He owns "the cattle on a thousand hills" (Psalm 50:10 NKJV). Surely if we have a need, He will meet it. We must be discerning, though, in what is a need and what is a desire.

If God believes it will be beneficial for us, believe it will come to pass. It may not be right away. But with God, the timing is always perfect.

May 18

At this stage of my life I have learned that you never know what tomorrow will bring. I, and many others, have experienced great sadness as loved ones suddenly die or are diagnosed with devastating illnesses. Without God in these times, people will fall apart. With Him, it is still difficult. But by His strength, we will overcome and persevere through the heartaches of life.

He is the rock that we lean upon.

He is the rainbow through the rain.

When we are in the valley, He lifts us to the mountaintop.

He helps us to smile again.

When darkness casts its shadows across your path, He is the light that will illuminate the way.

On Christ, the solid rock I'll stand. All other ground is sinking sand.

May 19

"You just aren't believing hard enough! Use your faith!"
These were the words expressed to me by friends and
acquaintances during my years of battling depression.

"What am I doing wrong, Lord?" I'd ask again and
again.

"If I just pray and believe hard enough, go to
enough healing seminars, I will be healed," I told myself.

Countless times I begged the Lord to take this thorn.

"Praise Him and thank Him for your healing in
advance, fast and pray."

Nothing worked!

Would you think less of a God who chooses to
provide the necessary strength for each day—as he did by
providing manna to the Israelites while they wandered in
the desert? That would mean total reliance on Him every
day of every year—no instant healing, no parting of the
waters; just believing for His touch, day by day.

In retrospect I see God has been there the entire
time.

"My grace is sufficient for you," He says in 2
Corinthians 12:9 (NKJV). He provides strength for the
journey.

I was not healed from depression. But depression
did not conquer me. I can honestly say that through it all, I
am solely dependent on God to do what He will with my
life.

I am here to say that, even if you are not healed,
God is still in control and He loves you immensely.

May 20

Greater love has no one than this, that one lay down his life
for his friends.
John 15:13 (NASB)

He who bore the cross,

Took the pain,

Felt the hate,

Endured the shame.

King of kings,

Lord of lords,

Gave up His life,

It's why He was born.

He gave it all at Calvary,

He did it all for you and me.

His life, His love,

At great expense,

He paid the price,

For all our sins.

The debt is paid,

Now we are free,

Heaven is home,

Death has no sting.

May 21

The intensity of the struggle is equivalent to the measure of victory at breakthrough. This battle is real. Your enemy knows who you are, and there is a price on your head. But do not let that bother you. God is in your corner and He will fight ferociously for you.

I believe the devil can see the vision God has for your life. He would not bother you if you did not pose a threat to the kingdom of darkness. Let me encourage you to be relentless in your pursuit for your God-given rights. Do it with boldness and confidence, knowing your success is in very capable hands. Do not look at the fiery trial, look to the author and developer of your faith.

Press on and fight the good fight of faith. The victory banner awaits. Never ever give up!

May 22

There are many people we encounter regularly in life, particularly in a work environment, who could be described as "difficult people." No matter how we try to get along with these people, they always seem to have a problem with us. I believe getting along with these people can be as challenging as it would be to hug a porcupine.

Sometimes love means we have to set a boundary. The Bible says, "Keep your heart with all diligence, for out of it spring the issues of life" (Proverbs 4:23 NKJV). We can love people with the love of God, but not give them license to walk on us.

God will give us all the wisdom, grace, and peace to withstand any situation if we submit our everyday problems to Him. How do we love a porcupine? From a distance, and gently—very gently!

May 23

Walking through total darkness can be unsettling and frightening. You have no sense of boundaries. You search, with arms extended, hoping to find something solid to grasp onto—a wall if you will.

Suddenly you see a light. Now it may be the size of a pinhead, but it is a light just the same. You are no longer without direction. You are no longer without hope.

As you get closer, the light grows bigger and brighter. You believe you are coming out the darkness into the day. You feel encouraged. You are hopeful. You are no longer afraid.

Jesus is the light for the world to follow. No one needs to walk in darkness any longer.

Again Jesus spoke to them, saying, "I am the light of the world. Whoever follows me will not walk in darkness, but will have the light of life."
John 8:12 (ESV)

May 24

There are endless tombs holding the remains of those who claimed to be a god. But, let me tell you something about our Savior: He is very much alive!

Jesus's journey did not end at the cross. It was not over at the tomb. It was only the beginning of an infinite ministry that will never lose its effectiveness. That *dunamis* (explosive) power lives on through all time!

To better understand the love of God, one must look to the cross. It is God's own love letter to His children: "For He made Him who knew no sin to be sin for us, that we might become the righteousness of God in Him" (2 Corinthians 5:21 NKJV).

The spotless lamb of the Almighty sent His only begotten Son to pay the ransom for our sins forever! God turned His back on the face of Jesus, so we may have the opportunity to live in eternity with Him.

That you may have the power and be strong to apprehend and grasp with all the saints [God's devoted people, the experience of that love] what is the breadth and length and height and depth [of it]; [That you may really come] to know [practically, through experience for yourselves] the love of Christ, which far surpasses mere knowledge [without experience]; that you may be filled [through all your being] unto all the fullness of God [may have the richest measure of the divine Presence, and become a body wholly filled and flooded with God Himself]!
Ephesians 3:18–19 (AMPCE)

May 25

"Today is the first day of the rest of your life!" This was an expression often used years ago, but I thought it appropriate for today's message.

Many struggle with meeting the day on a positive note. But today is a new day! God promises us a stream in the desert. He says He creates a new beginning every day. We all have the opportunity to be upset, depressed, and sad. Life gives us many reasons to feel bad. But we can make a choice to be happy. If you wake up and you feel the dark cloud of doom and gloom about to ascend upon you, just say "No!"

No matter what the reason, faith is often ignited with a smile or a "Yes, I can!" God works best when we have an open mind to embracing the positive.

It's a new day, and no matter what, we are still blessed!

See, I am doing a new thing! Now it springs up…. I am making a way in the wilderness and streams in the wasteland.

Isaiah 43:19 (NIV)

May 26

Driving to a friend's house one day, I realized I knew only one way to get to her street. But as it turned out, it was not even the right way. I suddenly thought of my friend, and it occurred to me how many routes she would know after having lived there for many years. It was then, Lord, that You brought to my mind about preparing, being equipped in this life. If I had asked my friend for an alternate way, I would not have been lost at that point.

Sometimes it's that way with Your children, Lord. The Bible contains all of the answers to life's questions, if I only knew Your Word. The better I know Your Word, the more equipped I am to deal with the struggles of life. Writing the Word on the tablets of my heart, ingraining it into my spirit, will prepare me for any storm that comes along. Utilizing the Scriptures will direct my paths toward the ultimate route for me. There will be no dead ends, no wrong turns. I will never lose my way with You as my navigator.

May 27

In the darkness we grasped the rags that held us.

We tugged and taped.

Parts wore thin and fell from our reach.

Soon the very heat that burned hot,

Helped fuse us together,

Becoming our strength.

Some who joined us for this life told tales of it being fun,
fast, furious;

They never said we would have to be steel.

We carry a mark on our heads the day we are born.

God put it there.

We will be brought through dark valleys and flames will
lick at our heels.

But our legacy will only be evident when we utilize our
ability to overcome through Christ.

"I will give them the courage as they choose to give Me
their life."

May 28

Jesus was counter-culture in his time. The Pharisees and their kind lived by tradition. Every aspect of their life revolved around rituals and conformity to those rituals. Jesus's unique ways threatened and shook the very core of their religious doctrines. Jesus was a radical, and they were terrified of Him. Jesus healed the sick on the Sabbath, He ate before performing the ceremonial washing of hands, and He dined with tax collectors and women of questionable character.

With God it is all about the heart! He used the seemingly lowest of men to do the most vital things. Why? Because of who they were? No. He used them because of the great heart He knew they possessed.

In Psalm 51: (AMPCE), David prayed, "Create in me a clean heart, O God, and renew a right, persevering, and steadfast spirit within me." I want to be someone like David. He made plenty of mistakes, yes, but God called him a man after His own heart. WOW!

Let us ask God to help us achieve Jesus's "heart condition." We serve a God who supersedes any lack we may be suffering in our lives in regard to our hearts. The Bible says, "Greater is He who is in you than he who is in the world" (1 John 4:4 NASB). Amen!

May 29

As the woman approached the town of the prophet, to tell of the news of her beloved son's death, the prophet sent his messenger to meet her:

And it came to pass, when the man of God saw her afar off, that he said to Gehazi his servant, Behold, yonder is that Shunammite: Run now, I pray thee, to meet her, and say unto her, Is it well with thee? is it well with thy husband? is it well with the child? And she answered, It is well.
2 Kings 4:25–26 (KJV)

This woman who endured lifelong struggles of death, famine, and intense hardship had the bold faith, against all odds, to believe her son would be raised up from his deathbed.

Attempts were made with the prophet's staff to bring the boy back to life. It did not work. But this woman was relentless in her belief of her son being raised up. Finally Elisha had to come to her home and the boy was brought back to life.

The precursor to this miracle was extreme faith. If we read the entire chapter, we will see the woman sacrificed for God. When her miracle of having a child manifested, she knew it was God.

She also knew when the child had died, it was up to God to raise him up. Oh to have the faith to believe for the dead to be raised and the confidence to declare under the worst of circumstances, "It is well!"

May 30

Sometimes God uses unusual ways to talk to me. A few years ago I was going through a lowly season, and I opened a fortune cookie which read, "Halleluiah!" I felt astounded, as I'd never seen a quote from a fortune cookie like that.

Do I think there is some mystical power in fortune cookies? Not at all! But I believe God sometimes will use anything to reach out and touch someone.

My first "God wink" from a fortune cookie came with the saying "Life is a wiggle, not a struggle." When I received this quote, I was going through a personal struggle. I felt as if God was saying, "Life is how you perceive it."

Just as a baby chick needs to put forth great effort to hatch, we too must endure turbulent times to grow. As a caterpillar spins within its chrysalis, awaiting a season when it will grow wings and take flight, God will utilize our struggles—while encouraging us—to morph us into His beautiful butterfly.

May 31

As I stood and prayed by the bedside of a dear friend whose body was surrendering to cancer, I believed God is good all the time—and I still do.

No matter what happens to us in this lifetime, God is gracious, merciful, and a healer. Sometimes healing does not come in this life. But as we enter heaven and are welcomed by our Lord, we are reborn into a new eternal life. With a new us, without sickness or torment, we are just beginning to live out forever in a place of utter perfection.

The sorrows and pain in this lifetime are minuscule when compared to the glory and wonderment of an eternity in heaven.

June 1

The apostle Paul of the New Testament came to know the peace of God that surpasses all understanding. His life was one of extreme hardship. He was often persecuted, or in prison, because of His stand for Jesus Christ.

It is said that he wrote most of the books of the New Testament while he was incarcerated. Yet the books he authored were quite encouraging and uplifting.

As we struggle just making it through bad days, we may wonder how Paul did it. I believe the key was his total dependence on the Lord. Paul had no other choice but rely solely on God to get him through the dark times. He had nothing else.

Desperation can be a precursor to building faith. As we endure the hard times, let us hold fast to the Word and cling to the Lord, who will provide strength and our answers in due season.

I know what it is to be in need, and I know what it is to have plenty. I have learned the secret of being content in any and every situation, whether well fed or hungry, whether living in plenty or in want. I can do all this through him who gives me strength.
Philippians 4:12–13 (NIV)

June 2

Lodebar was a place referenced in 2 Samuel 9 in the Bible. The meaning behind "Lodebar" is pastureless and lifeless. After reading about Lodebar, my opinion is that it was a place of last resort.

Strangely I thought of this life lesson when I was struggling to keep my old cell phone alive. It was an old iPhone and every time I looked at it, the power bar was low, or in the red. I spent a lot of time recharging it, because I used my phone to write and store devotional messages for the day. It was often in the process of writing these messages that the phone would shut down.

The thought of getting another phone meant losing all my notes and data. But I finally pressed past the fear and purchased a newer iPhone. I was soooo stoked as I entered in my iPhone password and, boom, all my data was transferred.

Likewise so many of us are living in a virtual "Lodebar" of our own making. But God's Word says: "See, I am doing a new thing! Now it springs up; do you not perceive it? I am making a way in the wilderness and streams in the wasteland" (Isaiah 43:19 NIV).

If we are to learn one lesson, let us glean this from God's Word: "Beloved, I pray that you may prosper in all things and be in health, just as your soul prospers" (3 John 2 NKJV).

June 3

I choose love!

Today I made my choice.

I choose silence when my words are not kind.

I will prefer His light when darkness tries to cover and
hide.

This world has many shadows and dark alleys. But I will
bring my light to the valleys.

I will push the yes button, I will give up the no. I will
always choose love, I will let my love show.

Love covers a multitude of all of our sins,

Let the goodness come out, so the darkness can't win.

As we place our trust in God and rest in His peace,
He will assist us with all the concerns of our lives. We can
go through the storms and survive, unscathed. Jesus Christ
is our strength, our shield, and our joy. With Him as our
ally, we cannot lose.

June 4

Stand in the water and let the waves of His love wash over
you.

Allow Him to immerse you and cleanse you from all the
bondages of this life.

Bring all concerns that weigh you down and let them sail
away with the tide of His redeeming love.

Let loose the clenched fists of anguish and pass it all over
to Jesus.

The moment is now.

The burden-bearer will trade you beauty for ashes and joy
for your sorrows.

Do not focus on the past, or dread what is to come.

Just breathe and say "Jesus!"

And my God shall supply all your need according to his
riches in glory by Christ Jesus.

Philippians 4:19 (NKJV)

June 5

Oh the many nights we lay awake in our beds, paying vigil to our worries. But why do we often do this when we can give all of our cares over to God. He is up all night anyway!

God is more than capable of handling EVERYTHING! Worry does not add one single moment to our lives. In fact stress is linked to many of the leading causes of death!

So why do we do it? I believe Satan is continually working to beset us from our goal of having faith. You see, if he cannot take our salvation, he will try to take our joy.

When I think of all the days and nights I've wasted on being anxious and fearful, I could just scream! So I am turning over a new leaf by constantly turning my thoughts toward God.

When worries come to mind and cause me to fret, I just say "Jesus!" When the enemy hears that name, he runs in terror!

We have the victory in our Jesus!

Thou wilt keep him in perfect peace, whose mind is stayed

on thee: because he trusteth in thee.

Isaiah 26:3 (KJV)

June 6

What wonders there are to witness in Jesus! All His magnificence we may behold in His redeeming power.

He takes whom the world labels "useless" and gives them strength and purpose. The throwaways of society are precious in His sight. Those who are brought low, He shall beckon to the mountaintop. He prays over them and, in glorious splendor, breathes upon their hearts a blessing of renewal. The vestiges of oppression fall away as He leads the procession to higher ground. What once was blackest darkness transforms to the whitest snow. The humble are brought to the summit and in union, all rejoice in His converting love.

"Come now, and let us reason together," says the LORD, "though your sins are like scarlet, they shall be as white as snow; though they are red like crimson, they shall be as wool."

Isaiah 1:18 (NKJV)

June 7

Hello, My child. Something told me I would hear from you.

You have been troubled. This I know. I can feel your every emotion because I created you, inside and out. Before you were formed, I knew you. You have walked your own way and it has taken you farther than you thought you'd ever go. You have felt unworthy to return to Me. It's okay; you can come back now. Do not ever hesitate to lay it all down at My feet. My grace is sufficient to cover every sin.

I have beckoned you time and again. I would hear you say, "I'll pray later," when all the while I was waiting for you. I do not say this to cause you sorrow. I want you to know that My mercy is endless and My love for you is boundless. I won't love you any less for what you confess.

I gave it all to prove there is nothing I wouldn't do for you.

June 8

Never, ever give up!

When you are at the end of your rope and everything seems like it is going wrong, hold on! God will not quit on you! Maybe others have hurt you, disappointed you, deceived you, but know this: He is faithful and He will never relax His hold on you!

Just tell Him what is troubling you and He will get you through this!

Dear Lord, thank You for Your faithfulness and love. Help us to forgive those who have hurt us. We bring all our problems to You. We believe You are working on these concerns now. You have the best answer to all our questions. We love You! In Jesus's name, amen.

June 9

We may think that all our struggles are in vain. But God will use those painful events in our lives as springboards to victory, if we allow Him.

It is not easy to feel hurt, pain, or anger. Giving it all over to Him means letting go of the emotions attached. It means surrendering by saying, "God, I don't know what to do anymore. I need Your help."

He is our refuge and fortress, our very present help in times of need. Give it all over to Him. The burden-bearer is in the business of taking the weight off our shoulders.

June 10

Come to His loving table,
All you are welcome here,
Enjoy all the gifts He offers,
He waits for His children there.
The table is ever ready,
It seats countless guests every day,
Your chair is always open,
You need not reserve your space.
Taste all the fruits of His Spirit,
Kindness and peace, He gives,
Joy beyond measure, is waiting,
If you only will sup with Him.
There are days when the seats are empty,
There are times He sits there with few,
But He never clears the table,
He waits at the table for you.

O taste and see that the Lord [our God] is good!
Psalm 34:8 (AMPC

June 11

Life is full of uncertainty. As sure as the wind blows and you know not where it goes, we cannot control our future.

But what we can control is who navigates, orders, and designs our life. Just as sure as we are breathing, the Master is in control of our destiny.

He is our light, our beacon, our harbor when days seem like night, and all hopes are dashed.

Storms may come, but nothing escapes His steady gaze. With Jesus in, around, beside us, we will prevail!

Though the water is rough and the darkness prevail, He will set our course straight and bring His beloved home safe and sound.

June 12

I think one of the most difficult things to overcome, more than forgiving others, is forgiving ourselves. We are much more critical of our mistakes than we are of another's. We beat up, condemn, and persecute ourselves far beyond what we would allow others (no matter how evil they are) to be punished.

Self-condemnation takes on many disguises and is ruthless at plucking the life out of someone who is under its power. Guilt, insecurity, low self-esteem, lack of interest or desire for better in life, complacency, depression, self-pity … These are just a few of the masks that self-hatred wears to keep us stuck and prevent us from experiencing any growth in our lives. All these emotions serve to render us powerless to making any positive changes and we resort to a mind-set that we are incapable of altering our thinking, thus creating an "emotional paralysis" of our own design. We conclude, "I think. I feel. Therefore, I am and I will always be." Lies!

The devil is the accuser of the brethren (Revelation12:10). He roams the earth like a roaring lion seeking whom he would devour. (1 Peter 5:8)

… but whenever a person turns to the Lord, the veil is taken away. Now the Lord is the Spirit, and where the Spirit of the Lord is, there is liberty.
2 Corinthians 3:16–17 (NASB)

June 13

The three days following Jesus's death on the cross, His body lay in the tomb. Many believe, as I do, that Jesus was not dormant those three days.

The Bible says in Matthew 12:40 (NIV): "For as Jonah was three days and three nights in the belly of a huge fish, so the Son of Man will be three days and three nights in the heart of the earth."

I believe that Jesus Christ went down to hell the moment He died. He appeared before the devil. He took the keys to the kingdom of heaven that Satan had held captive for thousands of years. While there, He spoiled principalities that had held many in shackles. At that very second Jesus freed our souls and spirits to the miraculous and the awesome life we can share with Him.

We are free from the old law. The law of adhering to strict practices to be acceptable to God was eliminated forever by the blood of the Lamb. He annihilated the works of the flesh by exercising power over evil: "I am he that liveth, and was dead; and, behold, I am alive for evermore, Amen; and have the keys of hell and of death" (Revelation 1:18).

We are now free to live for Christ and have power through Him over evil.

June 14

Do not let anyone and anything steal your joy! No matter what we go through (and I know it can be hard), just rejoice!

As gold is refined by heat, we are also purified under fire! It is intense! It is not fun!

Let us say together, "I can do all things through Christ who strengthens me." When trials come and try to beset us from fulfilling God's plan for us, make a choice to proclaim "Victory!"

Speaking life over circumstances diffuses the power of adversity. Believe me, I am preaching to myself! I have not arrived.

But as a diamond is produced out of intense pressure from all sides, we also can come out from trials shouting, "I am a victor through Jesus!"

Do not give up! Jesus always wins the battle! Greater is He who is in us than he who is in the world!

June 15

The voice of our God echoes sweet melodies of liberty. He sets us free, and we can know that it is God's power, His love, that has brought us freedom. We may see ourselves as weak. Yet God sees us as a tree whose roots grow deeper and stronger with each passing day.

Judging from outward appearances, we may not see the change in us. But our Lord Jesus sees us from a spiritual perspective. Revel in the knowledge God sustains us in all things and He provides abounding grace for us all when we fall short. He never looks at us and says, "I am very disappointed in you."

No, He gazes upon us through the redeeming eternal sacrifice Jesus made at the cross. Every time He looks at us, He sees the finished work of His Son.

He loves us 100 percent perfectly every day of our lives! How does He do it? He is God!

June 16

Many times I do not want to do the godly thing. When people are critical or hurtful, my flesh wants to rise up and give them a piece of my mind. Turning the other cheek is very difficult sometimes.

Rejection brings us back to a place where we feel vulnerable and afraid. Yet God still wants us to respond and react in godliness.

So how do we approach such a situation without feeling like a doormat?

Doing it for the Lord is the ultimate way to overcoming the desire for revenge. When this kind of situation arises and the flesh wants rise up, look to Jesus and say, "Lord, You took the shame, the blame, the hate. My silence is a symbol of my love for You."

Do I always practice this approach? No. But I am going to keep trying to exchange love for hate until it becomes a habit for me.

June 17

Many in the "garden of life" would call you a "weed,"

But I have called you to be a "wildflower;"

Whose roots grow deep in the hardest of soils,

Whose leaf will not wither in the heat and storms.

Some will cut you off or hoe you down,

But you grow back ever strong.

Man has not brought you to this place,

Nor will man take you away.

You will spread out and multiply

As My Word was spoken, My Word cannot lie.

I will take you to the higher ground,

For you were planted by the hand of God.

For he shall be like a tree planted by the waters that spreads out its roots by the river; and it shall not see and fear when heat comes; but its leaf shall be green.

Jeremiah 17:8 (AMPCE)

June 18

I have found myself in sticky situations before when I've begged and pleaded with God to get me out of them. Sometimes He rescues me; sometimes He doesn't. The times He leaves me in the situation are usually the seasons when He is helping me to grow stronger, or teaching me to trust Him more.

Most times growing in God is not easy. Nothing worthwhile and long lasting ever is.

I like to compare it to exercise. The first time I went to the gym, I got on the treadmill, my heart rate was high, and it was physically challenging for me to reach my goal. As I kept going regularly, my heart rate decreased and I felt physically healthier.

As we learn to rely on God daily, His Word promises us that He will strengthen us to withstand difficulty. The more we rely on Him, the more we will see that He'll help us in every situation to become the best we can be—to become more like Jesus.

June 19

God is the same, yesterday, today, and FOREVER! His Word assures that He will always provide.

Forget what the circumstances look like. Faith is the substance of things hoped for, the evidence of things NOT YET SEEN!

Jesus said, "Ask and keep asking! Seek and you will find! Knock and the door will be opened!" (See Matthew 7:7.)

Do not dwell on the past. The Lord said to me, "Just as you have a big windshield in cars and a small rearview mirror, you must focus on what is ahead and not keep your eyes on what has passed."

God will do mighty things in us if we utilize the faith He has deposited inside all of us. Today is the day to believe BIG for God!

This is what GOD says, the God who builds a road right through the ocean, who carves a path through pounding waves, the God who summons horses and chariots and armies—they lie down and then can't get up; they're snuffed out like so many candles: "Forget about what's happened; don't keep going over old history. Be alert, be present. I'm about to do something brand-new. It's bursting out! Don't you see it? There it is! I'm making a road through the desert, rivers in the badlands."
Isaiah 43:16–21 (THE MESSAGE)

June 20

It may begin with a breath, a whisper: the still, small voice beckoning us to draw near—not usually a demanding voice, but a consistent calling-out just the same.

The air is always present, yet cannot be seen. But we can witness the evidence of its existence by hearing the sounds of the wind, seeing the movement of the trees. Our God is omnipresent, which means He is always here, everywhere: continuously and simultaneously existing and attending throughout the whole of creation. Wherever you are, He is; with everyone, all at once.

We cannot conceive with our minds the enormity of a God whose presence is always present. But faith is what sustains us beyond what our minds can envision.

The Bible says that faith is "the substance of things hoped for, the evidence of things not seen" (Hebrews 11:1 NKJV). And faith is the conduit to plug in to God: "But without faith it is impossible to please Him" (Hebrews 11:6).

The best way to believe is to not rely on our senses to prove God is real, but just believe in our hearts. He is very real and He is always there.

June 21

The peace of God that passes all understanding is beyond our comprehension. In my own life I have only experienced glimpses of God's peace.

Jesus said in His Word, "Peace I leave with you; my peace I give you. I do not give to you as the world gives. Do not let your hearts be troubled and do not be afraid." (John 14:27 NIV). Years ago I saw an expression that said, "No God, no peace. Know God, know peace."

The absence of God in our lives means the presence of the world's substitutes for peace. The truth, though, is that anything the world offers for peace is only temporary and may lead us further down the road to destruction.

Let us draw near to God and He will help us to know what it is like to experience true *shalom* peace.

After all, Jesus is the Prince of Peace.

June 22

Many people live with the misconception that if they refrain from doing anything bad, then they are good. God wants you to understand the truth: if darkness casts itself out, it is still darkness. It is only in the presence of light that darkness disappears.

This world is a continuum of both good and evil. But our challenge lies in using our light, rather than focusing on the absence of the darkness.

The Bible states in Matthew 5:14–16 (NIV): "You are the light of the world. A town built on a hill cannot be hidden. Neither do people light a lamp and put it under a bowl. Instead they put it on its stand, and it gives light to everyone in the house. In the same way, let your light shine before others, that they may see your good deeds and glorify your Father in heaven."

The Lord has appointed all of His children to be "fishers of men." Yet many of us tend to be keepers of our own "aquarium."

Getting out of our comfort zone can feel very unsettling.

But, perhaps yours will be the candle that shatters someone's darkness. Be the one whom God can use to light another life and have His love burn in their hearts for His Name. With all of us aglow, we can create an inferno of love that no darkness can ever extinguish.

June 23

I used to dwell upon all the negative elements of my life. I often focused on why it seemed every time I felt like I was going forward, inevitably I would go backward. How weary one can grow when failure is anticipated!

Only God can change our attitudes by giving us a new perspective. One day, after I suffered a great disappointment, I said, "Lord, why does this happen?"

I felt the Lord answer, "Don't focus on thinking you had been going backward after you went forward. If you believe I bring only good gifts, then think of it as part of a dance. You are not just living, you are doing the cha-cha!"

June 24

Come with Me,

On this dusty road we'll travel.

When the dawn of life falls hard,

Your every dream starts to unravel.

The journey I will take you on,

Will bend you like a bow,

But in My grasp, you'll not break,

Soon My strength will show.

I, the archer and the

Shepherd too,

Who leaves His flock for one,

The master craftsman at the potter's wheel,

The fisher of all men,

The bread of Life, the great "I Am"

Gods own spotless Lamb

I've paid the ransom for your life,

You never had to ask.

June 25

You think you cannot hold on another moment longer. Your strength has waned. You haven't another ounce of positivity left in your being. Yet somehow you get through!

There, deep down within, comes that extra oomph you need to forge ahead, and you may even ask yourself, "Now where did that come from?"

My friends, our Lord makes this promise to us in Isaiah 41:10 (AMPCE): "Fear not [there is nothing to fear], for I am with you; do not look around you in terror and be dismayed, for I am your God. I will strengthen and harden you to difficulties, yes, I will help you; yes, I will hold you up and retain you with My [victorious] right hand of rightness and justice."

It is He who will pull us out of the pitiful ugliness of our life's circumstances and carry us through to a safe place. He promises us an abundant life.

Let us stay close to Him and not wander into dangerous, uncharted territory. He desires to keep us ever so close—not to be possessive or controlling, but to protect us from things, people, and places that will hurt us deeply.

His love is so precious, so powerful, so endless, and no matter how far or long we stray, His arms are ever open, welcoming us back.

June 26

My mother was one of the strongest people I know. She survived abuse, major depression and anxiety disorder, years of financial hardship, and relational issues.

In describing her I would say she was "rock steady" in her determination to be strong for herself, for family, and for God. But the day came when it was not enough to "will" herself through the pain. Eighty-one years of tough living can sure take the wind out of anyone's sails. Mom seemed to have finally lost her ironclad determination toward the end of her journey.

In looking at her most recent pictures, I saw definite signs of weariness. When it came time to see Mom's body after she'd passed, it was immediately evident that her spirit had long since taken its awaited journey to freedom and peace.

Before laying our Mother to rest, we had bronze angels standing sentry over her—one on each corner of her casket. After the day was over and the angels went to family members, I placed mine in a central location where I could look at it daily. No, it wasn't my mom, but it was a connection to her.

The other day I bumped the desk that the angel had been sitting on since the day of Mom's funeral.

Before I knew it, the angel took flight downward, hit the floor, and broke.

When I finally had gathered up all the pieces, I sat and cried. "It'll never be the same again," I whispered to myself.

The left wing was broken in four pieces and it had to be glued in stages. As I glued one piece after another, I thought of how in life, my mom had been a lot like this angel: shattered, but held together by a bond, by a strength beyond herself.

And now no longer is she broken. She is complete and lacking nothing. She ascended to heavenly heights where pain is no more and peace is forever hers.

Our broken angel found her way home. God has made her whole.

June 27

Surely as the sun will rise into the sky with the new day, disappointments will come in life. Situations, circumstances, and people will bring us pain. But even in all these things, we have hope in our wonderful Jesus!

He is a steadfast, driving force who will never say, "You're too much trouble. I've had it with you!"

I am so thankful our Lord will be there again and again! He is the Rock of Ages, and with Him I will stand. I place my hope and trust in the ever-loving Savior with the nail scars on His hands. Thank you, Jesus!

June 28

"Woman, why are you crying?" Jesus asked Mary as she sat at the empty tomb.

Jesus knew the answer, but He wanted to capture Mary's attention. At that moment Mary felt engulfed in the tragedy of her perception. Within seconds, though, Jesus would eclipse her reality by the truly miraculous.

It's Him! It's Jesus! she must have thought within.

The nail scars were the evidence of the great cost He paid. But there He stood, alive, shining in all His brilliant glory

Today He is just as alive as that morning He rose from the dead and exited the tomb.

He will transcend our reality at the speed of faith. All we need do is believe He can.

Transformation is His specialty. His business is the miraculous.

Are you His child? Then you qualify.

Now ask and believe BIG!

June 29

God will keep in perfect peace those whose mind is stayed upon Him, who love Him and keep His commandments.

How wondrous is the peace of God that transcends all human understanding and bypasses our logic. The peace that He offers is free, with no strings attached, lest you believe that following Him is a burden. Rather than an obligation, consider it a privilege to be of service to our King of kings and Lord of lords

The stage is set for your peace! You need not be prepared. Just say, "Jesus!" You now have a private audience with Immanuel, which means "God with us."

And let us, in the true form of a righteous servant, ask not what He can do for us, but rather ask, "Lord, how may I serve You?"

He came to save us—the lost and spiritually dying. How fitting it is to extend His message of peace to those who are in need.

June 30

Hello Friend,

Whoever or wherever you may be, I've just dropped by for
a visit via these written words of mine. I wish I could come
over for a cup of coffee or tea. Life just gets busy that way.
But if you ever need an ear to listen, or a shoulder to cry
on, just give me a holler online. I'll be praying for you in a
jiffy.

When they said life isn't easy, they weren't joking.
Who'd have thought we'd survive the roller-coaster ride of
ups and downs we've been through?

I guess we are stronger than we thought, eh?

Well, I know one thing for sure, I never could have
done it without my Jesus at my side. They don't call Him
"Savior" for nothing. I guess He's worn out many sandals
on His journeys with us. But He will never complain about
it.

Whatever you are going through right now, God
told me to pass this on: He's got you covered! It may be
hard, or scary. But He will get you through. Remember all
the other times you thought, *How am I going to get through
this?*

Guess what? You made it through!

I am not going to say it will be easy. But God will
be beside you, guide you, and hold you through it all!

July 1

The hurtful stings from human beings can cut like a knife,
Leaving a scar,
An indelible mark, Across your heart.

But know who you are:

You're a child of the King, you are royalty.

Don't boast of what you've done, it's all from His Son.
Jesus Christ, putting on the clothes of a pauper, left the
    Father's altar,

The heavenly place; Took on a human body,

His beautiful face showed emotion just like you,

He cried, He bled, He died on a cross, He is living proof
We no longer have to walk as orphans anymore, He settled
    the score.

When He said, "It is finished," He meant it is done.
Forever His blood seared across our hearts,
It has the healing power for all of those scars.

The battle cry to the enemy, he no longer has the victory.

The sacrifice was made, the price is paid.
The sting of death for those who rest in Him is no more, He
    won the war.

So do not walk as one who is fatherless, motherless;

He is the one we can place all our trust in.

No matter how you feel, cling to His Love, His Word, His
    truth, IT IS REAL!

July 2

The dark clouds rolled in until the sky was cloaked in a seamless ebony glaze.

Soon the thunder cracked and the rain pelted the ground with a persistent fury. The day surrendered, powerless in the storm's grasp.

The clock struck eight. All hopes of seeing a glimpse of light were waning. But suddenly a ray burst through the darkness, and soon, another.

No longer did the black horizon dominate. The sun in all its brilliance gave a brief but impressive show to signal darkness will never overcome light.

Remember how fleeting life's storms are. And no matter how dark and cloudy the sky, the sun is always up there, shining bright.

July 3

Keep and guard me as the pupil of Your eye; hide me in the

shadow of Your wings.

Psalm 17:8 (AMPCE)

David asks God to be as close as close can get. What a request this is! He is basically saying, "God, I want to be as close to You as being in Your eye. In fact I want to be part of Your being."

Oh, if our desire would be to be one with God— hand to hand, skin to skin, heart to heart. I know things would be much better off spending time in the shadow of His wings.

Healing came when people touched the hem of our Savior's garment. When we are wrapped in His arms, life is so much better!

July 4

Prayerfully proceed until He positively provides the promise! Many of us have goals and dreams for which we are believing God to bring to pass. Some days it may feel as though it will never manifest. But we must never give up!

A God-given dream is a goal that will sometimes stretch us to the max. We sometimes see this as an attack. Many times it is a test to strengthen us and cause our faith to grow. Many give up on the dream before it comes to fruition.

But God is not a dream spoiler! He wants to maximize our potential to receive the very best from Him.

Wait and expect His best! The vision is for an appointed time. Though it tarries, wait for it and it will surely come to pass.

July 5

Sin will take us further than we ever wanted to go. It will make us pay more than we ever wanted to pay. It will make us stay longer than we ever wanted to stay.

What can be the key to this dilemma? Jesus spoke these words to the captive who had been set free: "Go and sin no more" (John 8:11). Jesus knew that these ones who had been healed of a disease, or forgiven of an iniquity, would sin again. But perhaps He used those words to serve as a constant reminder that He is the one key to our emancipation from evil.

The staying power of Jesus Christ will break the power of sin and release its grip from us: "The righteous person may have many troubles, but the Lord delivers him from them all" (Psalm 34:19 NIV).

Jesus is the key to remaining happy, healthy, and productive for the kingdom of God!

The Spirit of the Lord is on me, because he has anointed me to proclaim good news to the poor. He has sent me to proclaim freedom for the prisoners and recovery of sight for the blind, to set the oppressed free...."
Luke 4:18 (NIV)

So if the Son sets you free, you will be free indeed!
John 8:36 (NIV)

July 6

God is huge! Try ginormous! He's bigger and stronger than any problem that may rear its ugly head in life.

Let's put this in terms of figurative dimensions. Mercury is the smallest planet. But it is huge to us as humans. So Mercury will stand for our problem.

The sun is the largest object in our solar system. That will be our Lord (although we know He is much more colossal in magnitude than that).

That's around 285 times bigger—and just to boast on His power even more: He made it all! So our problems are no match in comparison to His capacity for a resolution.

He who holds the universe in His mighty hands, loves us enough to care for every one of our needs.

July 7

The scene: Jesus is in a boat with His disciples. A storm is raging all around them. The disciples are in panic mode because their vessel is about to capsize—and they fine Jesus sleeping?

When we are in hyper-drive and our world seems to turn upside down, does it sometimes seem like God is not paying attention?

Beloved, no matter what the situation appears to be, never, ever believe He has forgotten you! People may have thrown you under the bus many times, but God will never leave you behind!

What's the price of a pet canary? Some loose change, right? And God cares what happens to it even more than you do. He pays even greater attention to you, down to the last detail—even numbering the hairs on your head! So don't be intimidated by all this bully talk. You're worth more than a million canaries.

Matthew 10:29–31 (THE MESSAGE)

July 8

How about those crazy days,
You just can't seem to get past the maze?
You are caught in that mire and muck,
The superglue has bonded,
You can't get un-stuck.
The days in the haze are just a phase,
The secret: get your mind out of the grave.
Do not let hell trip you up,
The trick is just do not get stuck.
He's messing with your mind,
Creeping in your life,
Playing with our brains,
Just isn't right.
But we got his kryptonite,
We will win, to be sure;
Devil, you are on the floor,
You are going to be sore.
Cause our Savior Jesus settled the score.
We may be down, but we are not out.
Jesus wins and evil is down for the count.

July 9

The one resounding theme of this life: keep on praying, keep on believing. You are in this for the long haul.

Remember this as you trudge through another day in the trenches: you are worthy of His blessings, His benefits, His promises. Do not ever think there is a clause that excludes you.

You are one of the family, a member of His "pack," and He's got a fresh batch of miracles that are there for you. Just ask and keep on asking.

He's counting on you to pray it through!

July 10

Good morning, child of the Most High God!

You are extraordinary! Do you know that? He knitted you together in your mother's womb, and you are fearfully and wonderfully made.

Never doubt for one moment that you are special. No one has your DNA. Your fingerprints were made for you alone.

God in all His magnificence has brought you to be, for such a time as this. He loves you with an unfailing LOVE! He knows your every emotion and sees every tear you've cried.

Never believe you are a nobody!

You are an original, one-of-a-kind, beloved child of the King! If you ever doubt it, just read His love letter to you, the Holy Bible. He has dedicated it to all His children and has inscribed His living Word upon our hearts!

That Word is Jesus! Let's love Him like we mean it!

July 11

Mediocrity is a mind-set. I used to believe I would never achieve anything in life because I felt invisible. When you spend your life traveling under the radar, just blending in, you will achieve what you expect: nothing.

I detested my lowly position. Yet I believed I was powerless to alter it.

Then I met Jesus.

You see, once you meet the Prince of Peace, a transformation is inevitable. He takes all the junk that the world has piled up in our minds and He exchanges it for gold—beauty for ashes.

Not one of us is an exception to His rule. We have an exceptional Savior who goes to bat for us all, every time. It takes a lifetime to transform our being.

Now let us say with confidence: "I am not a disease. I am not a nobody. I belong to Jesus. I am extraordinary!"

July 12

Years ago, when I was a new Christian, I was going through a rough patch. I kept beating myself up because I felt like I was always messing up. I could never be worthy and I considered throwing in the towel. Finally I called a ministry prayer line and spoke with a wonderful older lady.

I conveyed my thoughts and feelings to her and I remember her response even all these year later: "Honey, don't you know Jesus is like any good fisherman? He cleans you *after* the catch."

Her answer gave me a new and fresh perspective on being a child of God.

Condemnation is not something our Lord inflicts on His kids. He may convict us. but His intention is to educate and acquaint us with His ways. How very grateful I was to receive revelation of how simple God is.

We do not have to strain or strive. We just have to believe and let the Lord do the cleaning!

July 13

I do not think I would be presumptuous in thinking that we are all believing God for something in our lives. Some of us have been waiting for years for our God-given dream to come to fulfillment. I have to confess that I do at times get discouraged and even disgusted, and think, *It's never going to happen!*

Numbers 23:19 (AMPCE) states, "God is not a man, that He should tell or act a lie, neither the son of man, that He should feel repentance or compunction [for what He has promised]. Has He said and shall He not do it? Or has He spoken and shall He not make it good?"

Just as regular exercise builds and tones physical muscles, reading the Word strengthens our spiritual muscles, encouraging us to KNOW that God will deliver!

God does not want us to feel pressured to read the Bible. But He knows that our peace, the answers to our questions, and encouragement for our faith will be found there.

July 14

How did life go and get so hard?

I subscribe to being real. I believe that revealing all the wounds and the scars of this existence makes Christianity human and approachable. You see, we are all in this together. If I can translate that being Christ-like doesn't mean you have it all together, then I am doing my job.

I, like many of you may have days where we feel as though we are walking through the "valley." The pain is deep and dark. But, I can promise you, we are not without hope. We will get through it—because Jesus has forged ahead, to ensure our safe passage.

Hope is more than being positive. Faith is higher than just optimism.

Why? Because Jesus is more than the Son of God. He is our everything!

My prayer is that if you ever find yourself in a dark place, your first course of action is to call on Jesus—and to remember that if we were perfect, we would not need a Savior!

July 15

If you hear a voice that says anything like, "You're stupid, fat, short, slow, bad, ugly, poor, etc." make a choice and change the channel! The Bible says the devil is the accuser of the brethren (Revelation 12:10). So he will do whatever he can to suck the joy out of your life.

But Jesus said, "I have come that they may have life, and that they may have it more abundantly" (John 10:10 NKJV). God's voice is that of encouragement and love, always building us up.

God's word says all of the following about His followers:

- We are the head and not the tail—above and not below. (Deuteronomy 28:13)
- We are a royal priesthood. (1 Peter 2:9)
- We are blessed when we go in and when we come out. (Deuteronomy 28:6)
- We are a chosen people. (1 Peter 2:9)
- We are loved with an everlasting love. (Jeremiah 31:3)

Next time you are feeling down on yourself, make a choice and believe what God says about you. Just change the channel!

July 16

I used to try to be perfect. I wanted everyone to like me. When someone didn't care for me, I would beat myself up. If I did something wrong, I would be consumed with guilt.

Needing approval originates in rejection, and no one and nothing can fill the need except Jesus.

Realistically we cannot be all things to everyone. When the temptation comes to feel rejection, let us call on our rejection protection: Jesus!

By the shed blood of our Savior, God sees us as spotless, forgiven, and perfect. We have the ultimate stamp of approval from Jesus Christ!

July 17

Oftentimes the enemy uses the state of this world to beset and oppress us. Many issues today can feel overwhelming. If we continually focus on the negativity, it can prove to be devastating to our minds and break our hearts.

Jesus said, "In this world you will have trouble. But take heart! I have overcome the world" (John 16:33 NKJV). My hope is in Jesus. My happiness originates in His ability and willingness to help us overcome any catastrophe this world may be going through.

As long as sin is alive and we endure on this planet, there will be turmoil. But Jesus Christ is the Life Savior that never quits on us. Halleluiah!

... be satisfied with your present [circumstances and with what you have]; for He [God] Himself has said, I will not in any way fail you nor give you up nor leave you without support. [I will] not, [I will] not, [I will] not in any degree leave you helpless nor forsake nor let [you] down (relax My hold on you)! [Assuredly not!]
Hebrews 13:5 (AMPCE)

July 18

Countless scattered pieces of life cast into the atmosphere, strewn about, recklessly. With one sweep of Your mighty Hand, retrieved and gathered, You bring calmness—everlasting peace.

It's only You, God, who can make sense of our chaos.

At the Potter's wheel, You make the changes that may cause discomfort. Make them anyway, Lord.

Let us be ever receptive to Your direction and faithful to allow You to carry us through the storms as only You can do.

Lord, Have Your way in me.

July 19

Hey you over there, with the sad look in your eyes, it is going to get better. And I am not just saying that!

Be encouraged my friend. God said He gives us "beauty for ashes" (Isaiah 61:3 NKJV). That is not just a statement; it's a promise—His promise!

The world offers nothing but empty dreams. But those who hope in the Lord will never be disappointed.

If your hopes are waning, trust in the Lord and do not focus on how bad it looks. Troubles are real. But they are only temporary.

In the same verse mentioned above, God's Word says that He will give us "the garment of praise for the spirit of heaviness" (Isaiah 61:3 NKJV). Many times, after having a terrible day, I got in my car and put on praise music. Within minutes of listening to the words and singing along, tears began streaming down my cheeks, cleansing me from all the muck and mire.

I do not know what you are going through. But God does. Just lean on Him. He has more than enough power to answer all prayers.

Trust in the one who has the whole universe in His hands!

July 20

I believe that what lies in the center of the human heart is the desire to be wanted and accepted.

No one likes to be excluded or rejected by their peers. I remember that as a child I always wanted to be one of the kids who would gather, sharing secrets, even when I heard some of their whispers. Sometimes the whispers were cutting remarks, generated to belittle or berate those whom the "crowd" deemed inferior.

I am sure we have all been the subject of ridicule from time to time. As we grow into adulthood, the need for acceptance continues. Can we then assume that one of the key factors for motivating us to gossip is for recognition and acceptance?

As we age, our ideals may change. But our desire to fit in doesn't change.

The opportunity often arises to gather together and chatter. But if we resist the temptation to share in idle talk, it enables God to infuse us with His strength for future challenges.

Am I now trying to win the approval of human beings, or of God? Or am I trying to please people? If I were still trying to please people, I would not be a servant of Christ.
Galatians 1:10 (NIV)

July 21

When in doubt, cast doubt out! It costs nothing to believe in the power of God, and He has more than enough capability to answer all prayers.

He is eager to listen to and answer your concerns, requests, and questions. He may not answer your prayers when you want Him to or how you want Him to. But you can believe He knows the perfect time and way to do so.

If we allow doubt to enter in, it will grow and swallow up any hope for a promise fulfilled. Can you risk letting go of doubt and hold on to faith? Even if you've let doubt and fear dominate your life, you can surrender to the one who will change your world. Trust in the God who is sovereign over all!

July 22

I couldn't sleep,
A thought occurred to me.
It was raining large droplets.
I believe it's heavens tears,
They weep for those left behind,
They who really care.
The one who has transitioned
From this life to the next,
Shall experience perfection
As Jesus Christ greets them.
The eternal existence,
With heaven as your home,
Sickness and problems melt away.
Sorrows? There's no more.
The rhapsody of angels' songs,
Giving glory to His name,
Words they truly can't describe
The wonderment God made.
What we can only imagine,
As they are surprised and rejoice,
When they reunite with loved ones,
The laughter, the joy.
The sky had truly emptied out,
Yesterday, when she had passed,
Heaven's sorrows for those left behind,
Not for the one who had left.

July 23

Now to Him Who, by (in consequence of) the [action of His] power that is at work within us, is able to [carry out His purpose and] do superabundantly, far over and above all that we [dare] ask or think [infinitely beyond our highest prayers, desires, thoughts, hopes, or dreams]—to Him be glory in the church and in Christ Jesus throughout all generations forever and ever. Amen (so be it).
Ephesians 3:20–21 (AMPCE)

Think about this: A police officer does not possess the physical strength to hold back traffic. Yet he has the authority to do so. With one wave of his hand, he can hold back hundreds of tons of vehicles.

In the same way, God has given us authority in the spiritual realm. Yet how often do we utilize it?

Here is another scripture that illustrates the power we possess through God: "For assuredly, I say to you, whoever says to this mountain, 'Be removed and be cast into the sea,' and does not doubt in his heart, but believes that those things he says will be done, he will have whatever he says" (Mark 11:23 NKJV).

I believe it was a powerful word from God to show us that He will do huge things for us. All we need to do is ask and speak to our mountains.

July 24

Just this morning my mind gravitated back to a situation that happened several years ago, when God placed upon my heart to confront a complete stranger.

The man, visibly sickly and frail, was seated in a store at a flea market, hooked up to an oxygen tank.

I walked up to the man and relayed the message that I felt God wanted to convey to him: "Sometimes when we do not forgive, it festers inside and causes our bodies to weaken and become sick. God asked me to ask you to forgive today."

He looked at me with so much rage in his eyes and snapped, "Forgive? I will never forgive that woman as long as I live!"

"I'm sorry, sir. I was just passing on what I felt God wanted you to know."

About a year or so later, I dropped by the same store and didn't see the man there, but I did find his friend seated on the same bench. So I asked him where his friend was. He told me that he had passed away.

Sometimes God sends people into our lives to be His mouthpiece when subtle hints are not enough.

My greatest hope is that someone reading this will finally let go of some deep pain of the past.

Forgive and live again.

July 25

Lately I have been thinking about fruit, and how we can compare ourselves to it. If I were to be described as one fruit, ideally I would like it to be a Chambersburg peach. I recently had the occasion to taste one, and I have to say, it was like heaven—perfect in every way. The sweetness ... pure ambrosia.

Yes, I would like to be like that peach.

But at times I am unfortunately more like a sour lemon: bitter and not pleasant at all. Or have you ever had one of those apples that looked beautiful from the outside, but once you bit into it—blech! Mushy and no flavor! Or how about a grape that was under ripe? Yuck.

Oh how I wish I could be that peach all the time, lovely to look at and sweet as honey. But I confess that I sometimes gravitate toward being that sour lemon, mushy apple, or unripe grape.

But I am not done growing yet, as God is not finished with me. Because we were grafted into the true vine, Christ, He is always at work in us—ripening, beautifying, and testing our fruit until we are at our peak.

At times He may need to prune us a bit, and maybe even squeeze our fruit or use others to test our ripeness. But rest assured, He wants us to be the absolute best we can be so we can reflect His glory to the world.

July 26

I am the vine, ye are the branches: He that abideth in me,
and I in him, the same bringeth forth much fruit: for
without me ye can do nothing.

John 15:5 (KJV)

Sometimes I feel like a hot mess! I have had issues with anxiety all my life. I even experience times when fear keeps me from enjoying my life. Oh how I want to be free!

I still get anxious in crowds, and driving on the freeway sometimes sends me into a full-blown panic attack. I used to beat myself up over these issues, but now I try to envision these problems as a temporary place in my journey to healing—because I want so much to feel emancipated from the chains of fear.

That's why I cling to the hope of God's Word that says, "Where the Spirit of the Lord is, there is liberty" (2 Corinthians 3:17). I put myself out there in spite of my fears, in the hope that I can use my faith to believe God for big things.

As His word states, "I can do all things through Christ who strengthens me" (Philippians 4:13 NKJV).

So let us take off the limits and let God be God!

July 27

I think I can safely say everyone has been hurt by people. Many times, sadly, it has come from those who profess to be Christians. This kind of pain can really sting when a believer does something to us that's not at all Christ-like. One time, while experiencing such hurt, I felt Jesus say to me, "Get them off the cross! I died so everyone doesn't have to be perfect!"

I knew right away that I was placing unrealistic standards on someone. Christians are not perfect. We often sin and fall short of the glory of God. This necessitates our need for our Savior, Jesus.

He knew we would mess up, sin, and wound others, so He took the fall and did His ALL! The hurt is real, yes. But Jesus heals!

July 28

Dear God,

We know that You—who created life and light, Who constructed the universe, and who hung each star in every galaxy—can take care of us.

We repent, Lord, when in the midst of busy times, we become stressed and overwhelmed, and we take our focus off of You. Help us to keep our eyes of faith and hope fixed on Your face. Let us know without a doubt that You will perfectly align our lives in accordance with Your Word.

With blessed assurance we believe and stand in unity with the King of kings and the Lord of lords. You are life and breath, and every good and perfect gift comes from You.

We thank You, Father, for Your ever watchful eye upon Your children. In Jesus's name, amen.

July 29

I have to say,

I had a rock-bottom day.

Jesus, save me,

Pull me out,

I'm in the pit,

It's really dark.

Rescue my heart,

Guard my mind,

I'm falling apart,

Don't leave me behind.

I know You will lift me up,

Help me, please, to feel Your love.

I need you now, Lord,

Hold me tight,

Always keep me in Your sight.

Thank You, Lord,

You saved me again,

Jesus, my hero,

My life, my friend.

July 30

I will lift up my eyes to the hills—from whence comes my

help? My help comes from the Lord, who made heaven and

earth..

Psalm 121:1–2 (NKJV)

Beloved, this scripture proves our God is our very present help in time of need. Do not be downcast. Lift your head up and proclaim, "Help is on the way."

If the task seems impossible and the situation grim, look to Him who made the impossible! He made heaven and earth, and the balance of all are in His steady gaze.

God will supply your answer. He never will disappoint! Thank You, Father, for Your answer is always "Yes and amen!"

July 31

Don't get stuck in a rut! Many times in life we just feel we are in a "pit" season and it appears as though we will never get out. But God is faithful to come to our rescue, no matter how many times we are in the dumps.

We need to learn that feelings do not determine our reality. I used to believe that if I was having a bad day, I was having a bad life! I felt helpless to reclaim my state of affairs for the better.

I am still working with the Spirit to keep out of the mind-set that I do not have to go off on a rabbit trail of discontentment every time a dark cloud settles over my head.

The Bible says, "My God shall supply all your need according to His riches in glory by Christ Jesus" (Philippians 4:19). So He has what we need in our lives whatever we may be feeling or experiencing.

But our attitude determines our altitude. So to reach above the dark clouds, we must proclaim like the psalmist, "Happy am I because my trust is in the Lord!" (see Psalm 40:4).

God is faithful to deliver again and again, no matter what the trial we are going through!

August 1

Many days had passed and there seemed to be no break in the rain and gloom that had settled over my window. Then, all at once, the sun burst through the clouds and shone into the room.

As I glanced around the room, I noticed how dusty things appeared in the bright sunlight. When it was dark and gloomy, I could not see how badly the room needed cleaning. In my spirit I heard these words: *"Until we shed light on our circumstances, we are unable to see them clearly."*

With God's light comes awareness. Although our emotions cannot be seen in the physical sense, feelings still shape the way we view our outward environment. Like in my dusty room, we must allow light to envelop our senses. Only then will we be able to clear out the cobwebs in our minds and deal with unresolved issues.

Consider James 3:17–18 (AMPCE): "But the wisdom from above is first of all pure (undefiled); then it is peace-loving, courteous (considerate, gentle). [It is willing to] yield to reason, full of compassion and good fruits; it is wholehearted and straightforward, impartial and unfeigned (free from doubts, wavering, and insincerity). And the harvest of righteousness (of conformity to God's will in thought and deed) is [the fruit of the seed] sown in peace by those who work for and make peace ."

August 2

In writing on servitude to the Lord, I looked up the word and found that *servitude* means: "being a slave to; a bond servant" and "a condition in which one lacks liberty especially to determine one's course of action or way of life."

Logically speaking, no one would desire or aspire to become a slave to anyone or anything. But the paradox lies beneath the scarlet shroud of Jesus Christ.

When you sign yourself over to His care and become his bond servant, your liberty is ensured. The weight of sin is heavy indeed. The strains of a life ensnared in bondage are devastating, and many feel they have no escape.

The secret is hidden in the Master's hands. The nail scars are real and the contract is forever. Sign on the line and let Him take the burden. He wants you to stop trying to be strong. He desires to be your strength.

Lay everything down—one thing at a time, if you wish. But do it and breathe in the true emancipation of being a bond servant of Jesus Christ.

August 3

Sometimes we feel so weak. How fortunate we are to know that we can rest in the knowledge of God's strength. His Word encourages us to judge not the circumstances, but to walk in faith.

The trials of daily life cause us to feel weary sometimes. Then we are reminded to lean on His Spirit. Suddenly the day will seem bright with new hope—if we will learn to depend on God's Word as much as we need oxygen.

It renews our mind to all His promises. In hindsight we will realize the road we had taken has now brought us back to depend on Him.

August 4

Boundaries—wow! Where do I begin?

My sister and I had a conversation recently about how we grew up not knowing about building healthy boundaries. While instilling confidence and character in a child, lessons in boundaries will naturally occur. In an ideal setting the child grows up and possesses the tools to express "I'm not okay, or I am okay" with whatever happens in life.

But most of us from the "old school" were not given the tools, simply because our parents lacked the knowledge themselves. Many of us did not acquire the art of assertion with tact.

I remember years ago asking someone, "Why do people always get picked on?" The answer, "Some people mistake kindness for weakness." Ergo, we live in a world where people's meekness is perceived as an Achilles' heel to strike when vulnerable.

Oh, humans, where is God in all this? Let me say, He is right there in your spirit, whispering, "Be kind, be gracious, be patient."

Let this be our anthem: "God, help me to be the best 'me' I can be. Help me to be meek and kind, slow to speak and judge, quick to listen with my heart. And help me to not return insult for insolence. If I look like a fool, then I will be Your fool, Lord. In Jesus's name, amen."

August 5

Sometimes I feel like I'm way down there, living under His
    radar.
Like God's not noticing me; I know you know what I
    mean.
"Hey, God! Look over here!
It's me! Do you care?"
Then I remember those times when I went to hide.
It was You, God, who came to find me;
You wrapped light around me.
I was down and You said,
"Get up and take My love.
Whatever you do, never give up.
I will give you wings to fly.
To carry you out of the night."
Softly and so quiet is His presence,
So whisper-sweet, we sometimes miss it.
We are ever present in His sight,
No matter what we feel inside.
Take this hope and light,
Use it to cover your night.

August 6

I hope you smile, I hope you laugh, I hope you dance.

Many situations in life cause stress, sorrow, and a whole range of emotions. But even then, we need to embrace life and seize the day—carpe diem.

Enjoy then opportunities when you have a chance to laugh and smile together—maybe even to dance. The Bible says the joy of the Lord is our strength (Nehemiah 8:10). So no matter the trial, take the time to rejoice!

You are not rejoicing for being in the circumstance. On the contrary you are reveling in the knowledge that the Lord will get you past the pain.

So smile and know that although it's hard right now, you and God will get through this together.

August 7

Lord, in Psalm 103:3, You say that You forgive all my sins and heal all my diseases. I believe every single word in the Bible is Your truth. I accept and confess that the healing power of God is effectually at work in me, bringing about a cure in my body.

I also believe Romans 8:11, that the Spirit of God, who raised Jesus from the dead, lives in me. And just as You raised the Son from the dead, You will give life to my mortal body by this same Spirit living within me.

I stand in faith that every day, in every way, my body will continue to heal until every function is fully restored. Every organ, every tissue, every sinew, every nerve will come in line and function with the Word of God, and be healthy and whole, lacking nothing.

I thank You, Lord, for healing me in the powerful name of Jesus Christ. Amen.

August 8

As I am becoming more acquainted with God's love, I find myself also increasing in confidence. The more time I spend in relationship with Jesus, the more I realize just who I am through Him (see Psalm 8:4–6).

Many people in the Bible got a revelation of who they were in God, and by doing so, it changed the course of their lives and history too.

By walking closely with God, David conquered the giant, Goliath. Though he was just a youth, his faith in God was bigger than all the soldiers of Israel. With one shot from a simple sling, David subdued and killed the mighty giant. It was not by David's might or power, but by God's Spirit (connected with David's faith) that he slew the Philistine.

In reading 1 Samuel, you will discover God had been preparing David for this battle all along. In 1 Samuel 17: 37 (AMPCE), David said, "The Lord Who delivered me out of the paw of the lion and out of the paw of the bear, He will deliver me out the hand of this Philistine."

As you study the lives of Abraham, Moses, Noah, Joseph, and many others, you begin to see the pattern in their obedience to God and ascending to great heights.

August 9

One day I took an injured bird to a local wildlife refuge to be cared for. In doing so, I observed the various species being attended to. Owls, birds, opossums, turtles, and many other animals, with a myriad of problems, had all been brought together under one roof for one purpose: healing.

Isn't it kind of like the church of Christ?

We all come from diverse backgrounds with different hurts and issues, and we gather together looking for healing and love.

Christ is the one we can run to when the world rejects us. He will always welcome us with open arms and bring healing where it hurts.

As I was leaving the wildlife refuge, I noticed two volunteers freeing a pair of rehabilitated sparrows.

I exclaimed, "That is so wonderful!"

One volunteer replied, "That's the best part of my job."

Likewise, when we find ourselves overburdened by the cares of this life, we seek Christ as His ultimate goal is for us to discover liberty in His dwelling place. He waits for the day when we can shake off our burdens and discover freedom.

That's the best part of His job!

August 10

The tough times are essential for those who live for Christ. It is in those times when His children become soft and pliable in His hands.

You may say, "I can't take this anymore!" It's painful, yes, but vital. He is shaving off the calluses and sharp edges of our hearts. Soon enough we will become more desensitized to hardship, and we are strengthened for future challenges. Just as a weightlifter little by little adds more resistance to build additional strength and endurance, God can utilize the ever-increasing trials in our lives to build us up.

So let us be encouraged by our trials, knowing that the trying of our faith brings patience so that we can be complete in Christ (James 1:3–4).

August 11

You will show me the path of life; in Your presence is
fullness of joy; at Your right hand are pleasures
forevermore.
Psalms 16:11 (NKJV)

I don't know about you, but I want this "fullness of joy"
that David speaks about in Psalms. You see, I have
experienced brief interludes of joy in my life. But let's be
real: I hunger to be in a place of complete joy.

David said that in God's presence is FULL JOY! So
in order to obtain this great joy, we need to be in His
presence.

Well, I know what I have to do: seek His Face,
commune with Him, read His Word! It is only through the
Lord—for He is the Way, the Truth, the Life!

No matter what the circumstances around us, we
can have joy, peace, and rest. It is doable when Jesus is in
the equation.

So let's involve Him in all areas of life, and He will
invade those shattered emotions and make us whole!

August 12

The journey of life has taken me to a place in time

Where I never thought I would be, but I dreamed of just the

same.

Happiness eluded me and I often thought,

I would run out of life, nary tasting the spice

And bid farewell to the brief interlude of splendor that

merely teased me

With its presence.

Could it be, maybe ... never is now?

And I will not burst at the seams

Or wake from this dream

And discover

It was only a soft cover,

Enveloping me with its comfort.

Nevertheless I will abide in the bliss,

God's peace and happiness;

However brief or long,

I will drink in every drop

And just to be sure,

Periodically ask, "Lord, do You have this?"

August 13

Let it be said that forgiveness almost never happens overnight. The process may be lengthy, and it will require us to yield to God's wisdom. But if we obey His direction, we will be the ones who ultimately benefit.

As God has asked me to forgive those who wronged me in the past, He was subtle in reminding me of the many offenses I committed, which He also quickly forgave.

God may also ask us to go out of the way to be kind to that person. This is not to torture us. But rather it will serve as a conduit to His wonderful love, which is deposited in each of us.

Forgiving does not always mean we are giving the person a place in our lives again, only our hearts. As we humble ourselves in the sight of God, His mercy pours on us like rain. We forgive because He first forgave us.

If your enemy is hungry, give him food to eat; and if he is thirsty, give him water to drink; for you will heap burning coals on his head, and the LORD will reward you.
Proverbs 25:21–22 (NASB)

August 14

On the road to total restoration and wholeness, we seek to gather the pieces of ourselves that had been lost along the way. Life is a journey, not a destination. Through negative experiences, we tend to feel we had lost a piece of ourselves, our hearts, our self-esteem, our joy along the way.

Our perception of life, like pieces of a great puzzle, will create a complete picture of beauty if we take the time to give over the concerns to God. The aim is to gain a clearer perspective and insight into issues that cause our present lives to be affected.

It is possible to obtain through God a sense of wholeness (well-being and peace) within ourselves, and with our world, if we surrender it all to Him.

Many days we may feel hopeless. But God is our hope, and our redeemer. He never stops working with us if we allow Him.

Unlike an old, run-down building that is condemned to be destroyed, we are treasured by our Father whatever our condition—and God will never give up on us!

August 15

He is real, you know? Do not be afraid to test His ability to show Himself mightily in your life.

When you wake in the midnight hour, when worries take hostage of your thoughts, give Him the chance to transform your mourning into dancing.

I have witnessed the transformation from utter despair to elation as I've given my burdens over to Him. His battle cry is, "I will never leave you, nor forsake you" (Hebrews 13:5 NKJV). "Never" means now and forever!

You are not the exception, but the rule. Read the instructions—the Bible. God's got this!

Surely goodness and mercy shall follow me all the days of my life, and I shall dwell in the house of the LORD forever.
Psalm 23:6 (ESV)

August 16

We are all good at something. Let us use that "something" to do some good. However big or small, it does not matter. What matters most is we can make a difference to at least one person.

Be the kind of individual that makes God proud! You see, He loves us anyway, no matter what. But I would like to see a picture of something I did on my Lord's refrigerator—just like when my kids were little and they drew a picture. Bam! On the fridge. A good grade on their test? You guessed it! Now I am posting my beautiful grandkids' creations on my cool "canvas."

I don't necessarily think God has a refrigerator, of course. But I believe He has heavenly pictures and videos for us to see someday. Wouldn't it be wonderful to stand beside our Lord in eternity, and to see Him smile with pride as He shows us the things we did for Him?

August 17

It can come in a second. A moment of prayer. Or a song may play on the radio to bring you there. A time of grief, or a time of bliss, can cause the connection. And suddenly you are directly communing with the Holy One.

Although it may be but for a brief space in time, you know it is real. It is there in the atmosphere—almost a tangible evidence of His presence along with the absence of strife. Your very breath slows as you settle into peace.

He is here. Do you not feel it? He came to love on you for a time such as this.

Oh, that we could do more to extend the rapture of such a moment. But let us bask in this adoration, however brief it may be. If we never have this time again, we shall never forget when Jesus came to visit.

August 18

*I do not call you servants (slaves) any longer, for the
servant does not know what his master is doing (working
out). But I have called you My friends, because I have
made known to you everything that I have heard from My
Father. [I have revealed to you everything that I have
learned from Him.]*
John 15:15 (AMPCE)

God's Word says that we have the privilege of being His
friend. Let us reflect upon what that means.

When we have someone we consider our friend, we
talk with them regularly. We spend time with them and are
concerned about their likes and dislikes.

Being a friend of God is the greatest friendship of
all, because unlike people, He will never falter, never fail
us. Unfortunately we fail Him regularly. But He does not
condemn us or hold it against us. He loves us with an
agape love—an unconditional love.

I am so happy to have a friend in God!

God's Word says that as we draw near to Him, He
draws near to us (James 4:8). He gives us the option to be
His friend. He will never force us to do anything. But He
gently beckons us to come closer to Him, as He knows
being near to His presence is best for us.

He always is looking out for our greater good.

How blessed are we to have a BFF like Jesus?

August 19

I had a painful thought,

of all the sadness in the world.

The cruelty, chaos, and it was overwhelming.

"God help me," I cried.

"Help me to see something sweet and wonderful."

And God said, "Open your heart and hands. Smile big and
often.

Be a walking rainbow and share the love.

Be the someone who sees good in everyone.

Start by looking at people and thinking, *God loves them.*

Give more than you take and then give some more.

Don't try to do everything. Just do something."

So if everyone decided to do one thing to make the world a
better place, just think how much better it would be.

August 20

Years ago I had a tree in my yard that I just never really liked. Every time I studied it, I could not fathom exactly why the tree bothered me. Then one day, while I was outside, I asked God why I did not like that particular tree. I suddenly realized that one branch on the tree had all its shoots growing straight up. Even the shoots on the underside grew in the same fashion. It looked so unnatural and odd. But why did it bother me so much?

I could sense God conveying to me: *"People are a lot like this branch. In trying to obtain things in your own strength—instead of giving things to Me—you can become rigid like this branch. At some point, this branch was not getting enough light it needed and contorted itself to reach the sun. It is the same way with people. When you force things to happen in your own strength, instead of yielding to Me, You become rigid like that branch. You are trying 'to be,' rather than just submitting to Me."*

When we try to make things happen by acting in our own strength instead of turning it over to God, we are making ourselves the center of our universe. This is a dangerous place to be.

So then [God's gift] is not a question of human will and human effort, but of God's mercy. [It depends not on one's own willingness nor on his strenuous exertion as in running a race, but on God's having mercy on him.]
Romans 9:16 (AMPCE)

August 21

How dare he try to strike me down,

He slyly whispers slander and lies.

Does he not know to whom I belong?

God always sees through his disguise.

The Lord rescues me,

I call out His name,

No longer do I feel afraid,

When I lose my way.

He is the Savior,

Who keeps me safe.

No valley deep,

Or mountain high,

Is beyond His reach,

He hears my cry.

When I am down

And feel alone,

He calls me "Child,"

Carries me home.

August 22

We are living in extreme days! Earthquakes, hurricanes, wildfires, floods everywhere. What do we do when we do not know what we should do?

Turn to the one who has all the answers to life's hardest questions!

However you feel, do not let your feelings dictate your path and cause you to fall into despair. Let our focus instead be on the one who calmed the storms and parted the seas.

Let us include Him in all our cares and concerns, knowing the Bible says, "The LORD will perfect that which concerns me" (Psalm 138:8 NKJV). He wants to be in our loop. He stands by and waits for us to beckon Him: "Call to Me, and I will answer you, and show you great and mighty things, which you do not know" (Jeremiah 3:33 NKJV).

Lend Him your prayers and your ears, and wait for His response. It may not be His audible voice. But it will be knowing full well that our wonderful, awesome God is on the job, working on our behalf. Thank Him and praise Him for the glorious Father He is.

Let go of the heavy constraints that try to oppress you, and cling to the Way, the Truth, and the Life. Talk to God and let it go!

August 23

Solidarity is the word for today. Unity. Being joined as one. That, sometimes, is where we are missing the mark as the body of Christ.

I believe God would like us to focus on the positives and not the negatives in others. We are often quick to point out what is wrong with others. We do not focus on the good in them. As someone who was bullied as a child, I am making an effort to not be an adult bully. In social situations I observe that we often succumb to the pressure to gossip and bad-talk others in order to be accepted by our peers or to feel better about ourselves. I do not want to do that anymore. I believe God wants us to be loving and nonjudgmental.

We need to be a light in a dark world so others will look at us and see Jesus in us.

In the same way, let your light shine before others, that they may see your good deeds and glorify your Father in heaven.
Matthew 5:16 (NIV)

August 24

We have a heavenly Father who never gives up on us—although, from my personal experience, I can admit that I have days when I feel as though I am giving up on Him.

When I began writing a daily online devotional a few years ago, my main goal was, and remains to be, obedience to God and to offer hope through Him. In the journey, though, I have days when my own hope tank feels empty.

Recently I said to the Lord, "I seem like a hypocrite! Here I am writing about faith and hope, but it is I who feel hopeless."

The Lord continually encourages me to keep writing, keep believing, despite what my feelings dictate. His Word promises that when we give out of our heart, we shall receive. So do not give out of your lack, but from His abundance. It's difficult at times, yes, but we can do it.

Sometimes the troubles of this world makes it appear like we are standing on quicksand. None of us have it all together, of course. Yet we must not ever surrender, albeit how deafeningly the adversary screams "JUST QUIT!" in our ear.

May this be our vocation, this our quest: spreading the good news of Christ so that all will believe. Remember, no matter how painful the trial, He is never done with us yet!

August 25

Nothing you confess can make Him love you less! The Bible says, "For all have sinned and fall short of the glory of God" (Romans 3:23 NIV). Since the days of Adam and Eve, we have all been hopelessly flawed. But we serve a God who never gives up on us. No matter what we do, His love never quits.

Then, a new day, a fresh start, and we promise God that we'll be awesome this day. We climb out of bed—and all hell breaks loose.

Alas, the blood of Jesus is needful every day of our lives. Jesus smiles at us as we approach Him, and He says, "Here you are again. Come closer. I know you are not perfect. But you are perfectly loved."

What shall we say about such wonderful things as these? If God is for us, who can ever be against us? Since he did not spare even his own Son but gave him up for us all, won't he also give us everything else? Who dares accuse us whom God has chosen for his own? No one—for God himself has given us right standing with himself. Who then will condemn us? No one—for Christ Jesus died for us and was raised to life for us, and he is sitting in the place of honor at God's right hand, pleading for us.
Romans 8:31–34 (NLT)

August 26

I am sitting and weaving a new life for you,

A life full of blessings and love.

I carefully guide all the thread through life's loom,

I'm so happy because I love this job.

The thread that I'm using is silver and gold,

For you are precious to Me, don't you see?

So do not feel weary and do not get low,

I will carry you through everything.

The life that you knew,

The heartache and pain,

Is a thing of the past for you,

So stand and believe,

All things are changed.

Behold, I make all things brand new.

Put on the new nature (the regenerate self) created in
God's image, [Godlike] in true righteousness and holiness.

Ephesians 4:24 (AMPCE)

August 27

"When you work for Me, you never stop washing feet."
One of the final acts of Jesus, just before the last supper,
was washing the disciple's feet. This gesture of love and
humility was to be a lesson for us all.

The Messiah of all the universe took on the guise of
a servant to set a standard for His followers:

> "Now that I, your Lord and Teacher, have washed
> your feet, you also should wash one another's feet. I
> have set you an example that you should do as I
> have done for you. Very truly I tell you, no servant
> is greater than his master, nor is a messenger greater
> than the one who sent him. Now that you know
> these things, you will be blessed if you do them."
> (John 13:14–17 NIV)

And so our perfect Savior illustrated that no matter
how holy we think we are, we should always be able to
humble ourselves. We are to be servants and never believe
we are beyond helping others.

A beautiful example is Mother Teresa, who
displayed true Christianity. She served the poor of Calcutta
until the end of her life. She could have said along the way,
"I did enough. Now it's time to relax." But she devoted her
entire life to being a helper of mankind.

We cannot all be a Mother Teresa. Yet consider one
of her famous quotes: "Do small things with great love."

August 28

There is so much evil in the world. The darkness is insidious and tries to invade every crevice of this planet. But God is God!

He helps us to be strong and fight the good fight of faith! The Word says, "Greater is He that is in you, than he that is in the world" (1 John 4:4 KJV). We are strong in the Lord and in the power of His might!

So no matter what turmoil the world is experiencing, "We are more than conquerors through him that loved us" (Romans 8:37 KJV).

This is our confidence, that nothing escapes our Father's steady gaze. By day and by night, He is ever alert, for God never sleeps. How blessed we are to know that we are loved and protected by the King and Lord of the universe!

So we ask You, Lord, that the eyes of our understanding be enlightened, that the blinders fall off, so we may know the truth and it may set us free. Thank You, Lord, that You are light, You are love, You are power! Amen.

Yes, we have peace in the mighty name of Jesus Christ!

August 29

Loosen your grip on the issues of the day and take hold of the hand that cradles the world. Problems keeping you awake at night? Hold fast to the knowledge that God has all the answers to life's most difficult queries. He is in the business of making impossibilities realities, and He can do it for YOU!

Don't take to the notion that you are excluded from the blessings of God. Say these words with me, "Father, I believe in my heart that You have the ability to bless me. More than believing You can help me, I believe it is Your true desire to cause me and mine to flourish and prosper in life on earth as it is in heaven. These are Your Words, and I cling to Your truth, in Jesus's name, amen."

Now breathe and surrender to the steadfast, rock-solid Savior who will take hold of you, and guard you, and love you as though His life depended on it.

And it did!

August 30

This book of the law shall not depart out of thy mouth; but thou shalt meditate therein day and night, that thou mayest observe to do according to all that is written therein: for then thou shalt make thy way prosperous, and then thou shalt have good success.

Joshua 1:8 (KJV)

Alleluia, God is faithful! Let us draw near to God and know He is the King of the universe. There is no one like Him. We serve a Lord who bestows the greatest gifts upon His children. He wants to bless us.

In His Word, He says to us, "I have come to give you life and life more abundantly. Every good and perfect gift comes from Me. Draw near to Me and I will draw near to you!"

Thank You, Father, for giving us the opportunity, through the precious blood of Jesus, to boldly come to the throne to obtain mercy, help, grace, and peace! You are our Abba—Daddy—and there is nothing good that you will withhold from your kids! We love You!

August 31

I once heard this acronym for the word "fear": False Evidence Appearing Real.

I must confess that fear has been a major part of my life. I felt very anxious as a child because turmoil and strife reigned in my family environment. It is difficult to break a pattern ingrained in your soul so very early in life. But with God all things are possible!

It does not matter what learned psychologists may say about the human brain. God supersedes all known data and research.

Fear is indeed crippling and will inhibit us from experiencing true joy in life. We need to fight the fear through faith in God. As it says in 2 Timothy 1:7 (NLT): "For God has not given us a spirit of fear and timidity, but of power, love, and self-discipline." And in John 14:27 (NLT), Jesus said, "I am leaving you with a gift—peace of mind and heart. And the peace I give is a gift the world cannot give. So don't be troubled or afraid."

We are all works in progress. God is not done with us yet. So even if we face fear and anxiety day after day, we can remember what His Word says and know that He's working in and through us!

September 1

God is faithful to help all who come to Him. Though the world may reject you, or cast you aside, He will never forsake you.

Oh I am so happy to know our Lord is a God who loves us unconditionally and forever. He gives good gifts to His children, and He is not the author of pain and rejection.

Some people believe that God is a tough taskmaster who executes judgment against us the moment we mess up. But learning His Word teaches us that He is ever ready and willing to give His children love, mercy, and grace. Alleluia!

All that the Father gives Me will come to Me, and the one who comes to Me I will certainly not cast out. For I have come down from heaven, not to do My own will, but the will of Him who sent Me.
John 6:37–38 (NASB)

September 2

Lord, in solitude, I find Your solace.

One emotion, one prayer, transcends another.

I become aware,

Your presence awaits there.

I follow Your voice.

Your Spirit whispers,

My heart is full.

I surrender to the serenity.

The sounds of Your love

Echo ever clearer

And washing over me

Spills

Sweet refrains of Your grace.

September 3

The catalyst to overcoming adversity and finding freedom resides in the ability to recognize who we are in Christ according to His Word and then to let our words reflect what He says about us.

The Bible states that believers overcame the adversary by the blood of the Lamb and the word of their testimony (Revelation 12:11). The blood that Christ shed for the remission of sin is the same blood to help us overcome the world.

Nevertheless, without a word of faith spoken by us, God is limited to what He can do. Yes, He is magnificent; He is powerful. But our words and faith have to line up with His Word. Otherwise it is counterproductive to His vision. Remember what Joshua 1:8 (ESV) says:

This Book of the Law shall not depart from your mouth, but you shall meditate on it day and night, so that you may be careful to do according to all that is written in it. For then you will make your way prosperous, and then you will have good success.

If we are believing for breakthrough, but we speak words that say we are helpless, we will have what we say. Let our words be a reflection of our faith, so that we can allow God to engage our hearts and bring about the change we need within us.

September 4

Jesus said, "I am the way, the truth, and the life. No one comes to the Father except through Me" (John 14:6 NKJV). Alleluia! It is the truth that sets us free (John 8:32).

The opposite of the truth is a lie. Who is the father of lies? The devil (John 8:44)! The kingdom of evil desires to ensnare us as it whispers deceptive suggestions, aiming to take us captive.

O Lord, help us to be prisoners of Your hope! Open our ears and eyes to stay on the path that You have chosen for us. You are our beacon of light, our harbor of safety! Thank You for Your love and protection!

September 5

Sometimes the best lessons can be learned from children! While playing a game with my grandkids one day, I witnessed both of them have a meltdown because they were losing. I explained to them that games are not about winning or losing, but having fun and enjoying each other's company.

It then occurred to me that many of us often approach life with the same attitude. We waste so much time dwelling on the negative instead of enjoying the journey.

Let us try to change our view by focusing on the simple joys instead of magnifying the rough spots. God wants us to enjoy the ride!

The joy of the LORD is your strength.
Nehemiah 8:10 (NKJV)

September 6

*And how are they to preach unless they are sent? As it is
written, "How beautiful are the feet of those who preach
the good news!"*
Romans 10:15 (ESV)

No matter how I look on the outside, good, bad, or other, I
always like to have my toenails painted. I personally am
not a fan of toes. But when my nails are painted, they are
tolerable, I suppose. But more important are my feet.

They take me to the city streets. I see God's people
every day. I pass them when I'm on my way. I guess I want
to just do more than go in and out of many doors. I want to
brighten people's faces—show them what God's grace is.

For even though we all have sinned, Jesus's love
has called us in—invited us with open arms. See the word
"LOVE" in His nail scars. His hands, pierced so we can be
free; look down, the marks on His beautiful feet.

September 7

Many people hold on to pain, feeling justified because they feel they were the victims of injustices. Whether the pain inflicted was intentional or unintentional, it still feels the same. Pain is pain. It scars, it wounds, it festers at the core of our very beings. The ultimate tragedy is that the pain will continue to infect and inflict us—if we allow it.

Growing seeds of sadness and hatred within only serves to close the door on blessings and joy in our lives. If we recognize a painful memory as poison invading our bodies, continuing to rob us of life's very essence, it is likely we will want to end this destructive cycle.

I learned that being "right" or stoking feelings of justification at a suffered wrong does not help me sleep better at night. Being at peace with God does.

As it says in Colossians 3:13 (AMPC), "Be gentle and forbearing with one another and, if one has a difference (a grievance or complaint) against another, readily pardoning each other; even as the Lord has [freely] forgiven you, so must you also [forgive]."

September 8

In an earnest attempt to ease our sorrow, do we hastily apply our own balm instead of waiting on the Lord? I know I have!

God is much more capable of handling our issues and working things out for our greater good than we can ever be. In "fixing" things in our own time and with our limited resources, we sometimes tie God's hands. In addition, we may cause additional damage by making decisions impulsively.

An example would be if we had a bad breakup, and we jumped into another relationship to try to ease the pain. God is acquainted with our sorrow. He does not want us to suffer. But as we wait for His timing, instead of our own, He will cause great things to happen for us.

The Lord sees things multi-dimensionally, whereas we are limited by our humanity. God is able to determine what will ultimately bring us happiness and what would be detrimental to us. Let us lean on Him, the Rock of ages. In agreement we can repeat the words of Jesus in His sacred prayer to our Father: "Thy will be done in earth, as it is in heaven" (Matthew 6:10 KJV).

September 9

And one day I sensed You found me.

You know the pain that surrounds me.

I await the freedom from the chains that bind me.

Yet You remind me:

"I'm here!" You cry out.

When the dimness falls

And my hope fades.

My heart sinks in a darkened grave.

"Do not give up!" You hold on tight.

I'm boxing the darkness,

In the shadow of night.

Rescue me, Jesus!

Carry me out!

"I'll take your hand and show you how."

He has led me, carried me, loved me through.

"Your strength is in Me

And I am in you."

As dark thoughts provoke and are closing in,

I hear You whisper, "You are going to win.

September 10

Father,

Your light is glorious and there is no darkness in it. Sometimes when we are in the dark, a sudden light hurts until we adjust our eyes to it. Through You, illumination brings awareness.

In time we will experience the fullness of Your radiance, if we allow You to bring us to that place. Help to strengthen us with Your love, so we may be ready for the road ahead of us.

If there is fear, let Your perfect love cast it out.

Let us be children of the light as we journey on to carry Your brilliance to a darkened world.

May we continually lift You up, so we can draw all people to You. In Jesus's name, amen.

September 11

God is creating the ability in you to hold on! The days are tough. But He has made you stronger. With each challenge that presents itself in your life, God has created the opportunity for you to become a fighter.

He's raised up in you the tenacious ability to meet every challenge with confident expectations of a favorable outcome. Your faith has grown larger and bolder than those mountains standing in your way.

You remember the days when a slight valley of disappointment may have sent you into a pit. Now look at you!

Yes, you may be down, but you are definitely not out! The enemy of our souls and the principalities of evil have fallen by the power of your words, straight from His Word.

Not this time, devil!

Take it on down the road!

This kid is a fighter, and she's got the Lord in her corner!

September 12

Life and all its troubles can be solved with one name: Jesus!

First thing in the morning, before getting out of bed, let us give over our worries, our families, our lives to the burden-bearer.

Let us devote our first minutes of the day to Jesus. Just say, "Hi, Jesus. It's Monday. I do not like Mondays. But I am handing this day over to you—to make it the best Monday ever! Help me to stay positive throughout the day and to glorify You when things do not go my way. I give control of my life over to You now and forever. I thank You, Lord, for taking care of my business. I love You!"

September 13

A "Spiritual Bucket List" that we can all aspire to:

1. Seek to love the Lord with all our heart, soul, mind. (And remind ourselves that we're forgiven when our love is less than perfect.)
2. Bring as many people to Christ as we can. (And know that there are some who may not want to come.)
3. Be a great example of Christ by our daily walk. (And remember that Jesus still loves us when we fall short.)
4. Be successful in godly goals. (And don't forget that God doesn't care how much we achieve, only that we keep trying.)
5. Give until it hurts. (And always remember that it's not the amount, whether it's our time, talents, or treasures, but rather the heart behind the gift.)
6. Be a better person to family and those closest to us. (And recall that God knows we show our true selves in front of those we love most.)
7. Turn the other cheek. (Even when both sides sometimes feel bruised.)
8. Be faithfully optimistic. (Always stay positive).
9. Always speak the truth. (And don't beat ourselves up when we get tongue-tied).
10. Love ourselves, forgive ourselves, and be kind to ourselves. (While knowing full well in doing this that we can love others and have the grace to be forgiving.)

September 14

One day at a party, my daughter and I got to reunite with friends we hadn't seen in a long time. It was incredible that all those years in between did not matter in the least when we got back together. We didn't miss a beat. We just picked up where we left off.

Spending time with the Father is exactly like that. We may go days, or weeks, maybe years, without spending time with Him.

But as we come back into the light of His glorious presence, we can hear Him say, "Come on over! Pull up a chair. I've got a lot of catching up to do with you. Oh, by the way, you know I love you like crazy!"

For I am convinced that nothing can ever separate us from his love. Death can't, and life can't. The angels won't, and all the powers of hell itself cannot keep God's love away. Our fears for today, our worries about tomorrow, or where we are—high above the sky, or in the deepest ocean— nothing will ever be able to separate us from the love of God demonstrated by our Lord Jesus Christ when he died for us.
Romans 8:38–39 (TLB)

September 15

"I am a Christian!"
Those are not just words, my friends.
That says Who and what we believe in.
We need accountability,
People will take us seriously,
For the journey that literally,
Follows Christ,
His sacrifice,
In this we strive,
To be our best in life.
So no matter what we do,
Whether cleaning, teaching, or selling shoes,
Spread His good news,
But refuse
to do less than excellence approves.
100 and 10 percent more,
This should be the measure,
When they rate our score.
Because no matter what company you are working for,
Your true boss when you are God's kid,
Is God Himself.
When you make that sale,
Make sure you tell
The whole truth,
God is watching,
We have the proof.
The Bible says,
"They will know you by your fruit."

And if something is rotten,
This won't be forgotten,
If you say "I'm a Christian,"
Then your good fruit is missing.
You're accountable to God,
On and off the job.
Do not make Him look bad,
When you promote our Dad,
By doing the least,
When more should be had.
Taking shortcuts and doing less,
Is not His best,
Making 'splendid' your quest,
Then you can confess,
In the Lord, you are blessed.

September 16

The dreams of all this life are scattered,

Upon the vastness of the dark sea,

As God has hearkened one by one,

I see them coming back to me.

The tide waves rush in,

Torrent blows upon life's shores,

The mighty wind echoes the voice,

"Do not ever expect more."

But God will turn the tide for me,

The sea is in His grasp.

My hope in Him won't disappoint,

I'll taste victory at last.

*For the Gentiles eagerly seek all these things; for your
heavenly Father knows that you need all these things. But
seek first His kingdom and His righteousness, and all these
things will be added to you. So do not worry about
tomorrow; for tomorrow will care for itself. Each day has
enough trouble of its own.*
Matthew 6:32–34 (NASB)

September 17

But without faith it is impossible to please him: for he that cometh to God must believe that he is, and that he is a rewarder of them that diligently seek him.
Hebrews 11:6 (KJV)

Thank You, Father, that in seeking You, we find our answers, the fulfillment of our dreams, and our peace, our happiness, our love.

We love You, Lord, and in worshipping You, our love is brought to perfection. You teach us that perfect love, coming from You, casts out all fear. We can give it all to You, the "Master of Mending," and You will make all things new again. We ask this and all things in the mighty name of Jesus.

Sometimes it's so hard out there, Lord. We feel all alone, as though no one has our back, when times are tough. Give us rest and peace. Help us to fight our battles. Strengthen us with Your almighty power that resides within us.

We believe You will cause all things to work for our good. We stand in prayer for those who are struggling now. We proclaim we have the victory through You.

We give everything over to Your capable hands, believing You will cause all things to work for our good. We have victory in Jesus!

September 18

Look for ways to go the extra mile! We have to do many things every day to get by: work, pay bills, eat, sleep, etc. But then there are the extras we can do to make a lasting difference in this world: a smile, a word of encouragement, a "Thank you for your service" to a veteran, an extra tip for a hardworking waiter or waitress. These are things we do not have to do, but should do.

During one stretch of my life, I passed by a small office building on the way to work every day. I noticed they were building something in the corner of the lot. It wasn't long before the project came to completion. It ended up being a small pavilion with a picnic table and a large bucket for cigarette butts. It warmed my heart to think that this employer went out of his/her way to create a place where employees could take a cigarette break, relax, and keep dry. Some might say, "Well, they shouldn't be smoking." But I say that this special boss looked past judgmental reasoning and went the extra mile to show care for others.

Compassion is love in action.

September 19

Some reminders as we live out today:

- Be yourself, but make an effort to only exhibit the good that dwells in you.
- Do not aspire to be in the spotlight, but rather reflect the light of Christ within.
- Try to see the best in everyone. After all, we are all daughters and sons.
- Remember that God desires for us to give more than we take.
- Be initiators of hope and peace.
- Forgive and live again.
- Let grace be your style.
- We may not be perfect, but we can be better.
- Let's always try to give of ourselves.
- When our hands are empty, let us fill them by extending a hand to others.
- It costs nothing to smile.
- We can all be ambassadors of peace, so let peace begin with us.

September 20

I don't quite know how I can explain it,
I guess the best way is just to say this:
Remember the adolescent years,
The growing pains would bring on tears.
The pain you felt was worth it when
You grew another inch again.
In our journey that we take with God,
The times that we will find hard,
The silent days we wait on Him,
Yet in the silence trust begins.
The peace that comes from quiet faith,
His signature love and waves of grace.
The trials are tough, but you are stronger.
It seems like you can hold on longer.
The faith God planted, that mustard seed,
Has just sprung roots, He's growing me.

September 21

Not long ago, I traveled the path of the mundane, the mediocre. You know, the old road of "just barely getting by." Then one day, as I was running as fast as I could toward nowhere, I collided with the ugly truth: I was a wreck!

Many degrees of disasters exist, and I could only compare my life at that point to a "clueless-ness" of a catastrophic nature.

Many of us believe we've missed the boat on having a purpose in life. Someway, somehow, despite God's infinite grace and love, we believe He's deemed us "unacceptable."

But God is not moody nor is He waiting for an opportunity to "get" us. He is ever ready to come to our aid at any given moment. All we need do is ask.

To awaken our God-given purpose, let us begin by asking the simple question, "May I help you?"

If your hands are empty, hold someone else's. If you think that you have nothing to give, then give of yourself. If you are all alone, find someone who's lonely.

The Lord promises us in His Word, "Give, and [gifts] will be given to you.... For with the measure you deal out ... it will be measured back to you" (Luke 6:38 AMPCE). God also promises His children life more abundant "till it overflows" (John 10:10 AMPCE). What can you expect if you open your life and heart to Jesus Christ? Over-the-top, overflowing living awaits you. You can count on it!

September 22

Sometimes it is easy to dwell on what we do not have. But let us choose to celebrate what we do have.

We have a heavenly Father who loves us very much. He will never leave us or forsake us. Suffering may come for a night, but joy comes in the morning. He keeps us as the apple of His eye. He will not let the righteous be forsaken, nor our family begging bread. All of His promises are yes and amen.

We that wait on the Lord shall have our strength renewed. We will run and not grow weary. If God be for us, who can be against us? He has not given us a spirit of fear, but of power, love, a sound mind, discipline, and self-control. God shall supply our every need according to His riches in glory through Jesus Christ, and He knows those needs before we even ask.

These and many, many more are the promises of God, written in His Holy Book!

September 23

A beam of bright, white light,

to shine on through the darkest night.

The harbor in the raging waves,

The peace to soothe when we're afraid.

The love to mend the brokenness,

To make our lives all make sense.

To gather and weave the hopes and dreams,

To cast aside the least needful things.

The hope and faith for a better day,

The silver lining in the clouds of gray.

All this is possible, it will come true,

When you let Christ in to live through you.

September 24

*For the Lord will comfort Zion; He will comfort all her
waste places. And He will make her wilderness like Eden,
and her desert like the garden of the Lord. Joy and
gladness will be found in her, thanksgiving and the voice of
song or instrument of praise.*
Isaiah 51:3 (AMPCE)

God is asking us at this time of renewal and change,
"Where is your wilderness?"

It is essential that we recognize the primary purpose
God want to bring us to when we find ourselves in the
wilderness of life. Let us get a mental picture of a
wilderness: desolation, quiet, emptiness. Do you think God
meets us there so we may put aside all confusion and
calamity? Then we are able to quiet our minds to hear His
voice—His still, small voice. God is multi-purposeful in
His vision for our lives!

Have you ever looked into a diamond? Within the
structure of the diamond, there are many prisms, which
cause the diamond to reflect light. This is what brings out
the brilliance of the stone. Liken that to God in our lives.

He is the Master Craftsman who designs us to
reflect His light. As a diamond may have imperfections, or
occlusions, likewise we have flaws. But given over to our
Lord and Savior, we take on His light. When we submit to
Him, we become His work of art. He gives us His brilliance
and we are never the same again.

September 25

If God is for us, who can be against us?

Romans 8:31 (NIV)

Not one thing can challenge the power of Almighty God!
Even though the odds might be stacked against your favor,
and the opposition might feel insurmountable, the Lord of
the universe is on your side.

You've perhaps lost a battle—but you will win the
war! Good will overcome evil.

The proof is in the Book of Life. Yes, the summit is
high and the terrain steep. But He equips us for the climb.
You will stumble at times. The enemy will nip at your
heels. Stand firm and believe that God will bring you
through the fire. You can feel the heat, yes. But you will
come out and not even smell like smoke. The Redeemer
lives and He will finish your story gloriously!

He who did not spare his own Son, but gave him up for us

all—how will he not also, along with him, graciously give

us all things?

Romans 8:32 (NIV)

September 26

Oh, what a world! How did it get so bad? We live in a world where many are being used to destroy God's people. This has been happening since the inception of human life. Sin entered in by Adam and Eve's disobedience to God.

Just as soon as they chose to eat of the fruit, sin and corruption came to be.

It wasn't long after Adam and Eve, when the evidence of evil proved fatal between brothers—Cain and Abel. People ask, "Where is God?" when lives are lost. He is right there mourning along with the rest of us. But Satan rejoices, as his sole purpose is to steal, kill, and destroy.

Jesus gives life. Satan takes it.

I wish I could say that we will not witness anymore carnage, murder, or atrocities in this lifetime. But as long as evil lives in the hearts of men, the devastation of life will continue.

But let us not be afraid. We know who our God is!

Psalm 91 talks of His protection: "He that dwelleth in the secret place of the most High shall abide under the shadow of the Almighty.... Surely he shall deliver thee from the snare of the fowler, and from the noisome pestilence. He shall cover thee with his feathers, and under his wings shalt thou trust" (vv. 1, 3–4 KJV).

September 27

I once overheard one precious person, who was mentally challenged, say to another, "I love you, in sickness and health." I thought that was the sweetest thing to say.

The childlike heart is the heart closest to God. As we mature, we often lose our innocence and we build up walls to protect our hearts.

I want to have a childlike heart—a heart that loves at any cost. I know God's love far exceeds sickness and health, riches or poverty, and it reaches beyond death, into eternity. Certainly love can disappoint and scar us. But look beyond the wounds and reach deep within, to the place where Jesus resides. His is the love that never says quit! He took the fall and gave His all! That truly is a "happily ever after" love.

September 28

You were born to do extraordinary things! Now is the time to bring your game!

He created you for big stuff. So show your strength in God big time and make it count! It's your time to shine.

He is counting on you. He has filled you with His Spirit, strength, and love. He needs His army now more than ever. Do not think for one moment He can't use you. You are a mighty man/woman of valor! Take the shield of faith and the sword of the spirit and go!

The enemy to all that is pure and godly in the world is in the ring for another round. As soldiers of the one true risen Christ, we are going to knock him out! Today is your day. Now go out there like you mean business!

September 29

It's a feeling you get when all your energy is spent. The resources are bankrupt and you've already dipped into your inner reserves. Simply put, you feel: empty.

You don't cry out, but your insides are screaming, "Is there anybody out there? God?"

He knows the voice. He's familiar with the pain. After all, He's been through it all.

Then His voice beckons: "Have hope, My child. Trust now in Me."

Soon the problem doesn't seem so large; the burden, so overwhelming. He came. He saw. The shadow has lifted. We are seeing daylight once again. Our God and King granted a reprieve to us—never to be a convict of darkness again. We are now prisoners of hope!

September 30

O my Jesus,
What You did for us.
You lived to die,
You love us, why?
I cannot believe,
Can't conceive,
We're not deserving,
You made us worthy.
Oh how your love
Covers sin up.
The blackness turns white as snow,
Your grace abides in the blood that flows.
I am astounded.
You keep us grounded.
I was hopeless,
Gave up until
Jesus came and changed my focus;
Now instead of looking down
In spite of my "human-ness,"
My sights are heaven bound.

October 1

Can I tell you something from the Master of the universe? You thought you were done. But God hasn't given up on you!

Is that all? Oh no! Something much, much greater awaits in your future.

All you need do is say "Yes, Lord!"

He will pick up the broken fragments of all those years and give you "beauty for ashes" (Isaiah 61:3 KJV). He believes in you! He is confident of your abilities. You know why? Because He's placed His gifts on the inside of you and "God don't make no junk!"

As I woke this morning, I heard Him whisper in my heart, *"Tell them I believe in them and they can do all things through Christ who strengthens them!"*

The dream is inside you. You have the key to unlock your potential. All you need do is say, "Yes, Lord, I will serve You!" He will raise the bar, help you reach for the stars, and take you places you've never been!

October 2

Be still, and know I am God.
Psalm 46:10 (NKJV)

Let Heaven and nature sing, the Savior's come to earth,

God has come to set us free, the symbol is His birth.

Enslaved no more by sin and death,

The battle has been won,

God declared the debt is paid,

Purchased by His Son.

Oh come, all ye who have no joy, no light, nor possessor of

love,

The Light of the world is God's gift to you,

Rejoice! He has rescued us!

October 3

It may be time to clean out your "refrigerator"! A few years ago the Lord gave me an illustration when I asked Him why saved people aren't walking in freedom.

He said, *"You know when there is an odor in your refrigerator? You look in there and everything seems to be fine. But there is one thing hiding somewhere that causes the smell."*

People are a lot like that refrigerator. They come to the cross of Jesus. They lay down their sins, hate, secrets; yet there may be something hiding that they will not let Jesus get to. These things, like in a refrigerator, will cause decay in our hearts, spirit, and bodies. This is one way that the enemy can gain entry into our lives. Whether it is unresolved hurts, bitterness, hatred, etc., it must be exposed and cleansed by the blood of Christ. Otherwise the decay will increase and cause disease, a hard heart, or even turning from the Lord. Only God knows how to eradicate the stench in us.

So let's pray: "Dear God, You know everything about me. Nothing escapes Your steady gaze. I confess I have things that I've held onto. I want to let go of everything that would interfere with receiving You fully in my life. Please cleanse me from top to bottom and inside out so that Your light will shine bright in me. I thank You for cleaning me with the precious blood of Jesus, which makes me whiter than snow. I will continue to expose everything to You and not hide anything. In Jesus's name."

October 4

Things that make you go "Hmmm …"

It is so hard to comprehend that the God of all the universe is crazy in love with us. But He is.

He called the earth and the heavens into being. It was not enough.

He gave us plants for food and fruit-bearing trees.

He created the animals and proclaimed that people would have dominion over all creation.

God looked at everything and said, "Now it is good."

As if that wasn't enough, He created us in His very own image. We are made in the likeness of our awesome God. But when Adam and Eve disobeyed the Father, sin entered. We fell. We dropped the ball.

But God did not fail us. He saw His people were desperate and needed a Savior.

Enter Jesus. He came, He died, He conquered. Death and sin no longer have the power to crush us— because of the cross. What love! The weight of humanity's filth was heaped upon His shoulders, and He took it.

The spotless Lamb became the scapegoat for all time. He loves us beyond limits and offers grace for our failures. Ten thousand do-overs and then some.

Jesus is not an excuse to sin; He is the reproof of sin. He knew we would sin. But sin is no longer fatal. He did it for you, He did it for me, He did it for love.

October 5

Semper fidelis is the motto of the US Marine Corps, and it means "always faithful." In the line of duty, marines are trained to exemplify never-ending loyalty to protect and serve.

This would also be a great motto for our Lord: always faithful! He will always be there, no matter what. Unlike the marines, though, our Lord is not limited by being in a human body.

There is nothing, NOTHING Jesus cannot do!

He asks us to come to Him with ALL our problems, BIG and small, and He will get the job done. We do not have to ever feel ashamed or unworthy. It is the blood of Jesus that has placed us in the front row—right at the foot of the cross!

It is not by our efforts; it is by God's grace. None of us are worthy—not one. But we are accepted into His beloved family by the spotless Lamb, our Lord Jesus.

So come boldly before the throne and accept the inheritance of our Father!

October 6

In our daily travels we oh so often find disharmony and strife. We yearn for the heart of Christ, to love beyond the realm of humanity. We pray to forgive those who wronged us, by shaking off the weights of discord, but sometimes it all just seems too difficult and beyond reach. And it is—in our own strength.

The only way to love beyond barriers is to lean on the cross of Jesus. Inviting Him in to perform heart repair within us will breach the limitations set by our flesh.

I desire to set a precedent for myself in this regard. I want to raise the bar on my abilities to practice charity, forgiveness, and grace. I have not even started. I don't even know how to try. But I guess I will begin by asking God to create a clean heart within me. And through all the tomorrows I will ask again and again.

Dear God, we will love faithful and true when we learn to love like You.

October 7

Every day I try to maintain an attitude of gratitude. Here is
a poem of thanks I wrote to our Father who is so giving:

As I sat here this morning and ate my breakfast,
I said with my mouth, "Thank You, Father, for this!"
I never take for granted the food I eat,
the roof over my head, the shoes on my feet.
It seems the harder times have taken me to
A place of heartfelt gratitude.
The tears stream down upon my face.
How can I deserve such favor and grace?
Lord, this is not just lip service for me.
The road that I walked took me down on my knees.
I know there are many out there who cry.
I cannot help all, but I will promise to try.
When I cannot give food, I will offer a prayer.
We can know You will help us there.
I so badly want to be,
Jesus, Your hands and feet.
But I confess my flesh gets in the way,
So I just close my eyes and I pray.
"Help me, Lord, so I can help too,
In me, let them see You."

October 8

We are made righteous not by *who* we are, but by *whose* we are.

No matter how much we try to live perfectly and without sin, we cannot make it on our own merit. God's Word goes so far as to say that our own righteousness is as filthy rags before the Father (Isaiah 64:6).

We have a sinful nature. It is only when we give our hearts to Christ that we become righteous. As it says in Ephesians 2:8–9 (NKJV): "For by grace you have been saved through faith, and that not of yourselves; it is the gift of God, not of works, lest anyone should boast."

Salvation is not a reward for the good things we have done, so none of us can boast about it. Jesus became the sacrifice for us all. He was, is, and always will be the Lamb who takes away the sins of the world. His death is the atonement for every sin we will ever commit.

Do not ever believe the lie your sin is beyond God's ability to cover you and forgive. We cannot "out-sin" His grace. This is not to say we should use this gift as an excuse to live in sin. As we give ourselves over to the Lord, our desire should be to please Him. Yes, we will make mistakes. But when we do, all is not lost. God's grace is sufficient, and He is willing and able to wash us clean.

His Word states that He removes our sins "as far as the east is from the west" (Psalm 103:12 NKJV). All we need to do is to ask Him.

October 9

Thank you Lord for giving life and health to our flesh. We thank You for this new day. We rejoice and worship You. There is no one like our God!

We bring all our cares and concerns to the foot of the cross. Jesus, our Savior, our supporter, our love, there is no one like You. Thank You for paying the ultimate price so that we may be free!

We give You the firstfruits of our day to offer our praise. We love You, Lord! You are precious in our sight. Today we will focus on thoughts of You and not just ourselves.

Take us to that life-filled well and fill us up. Give us Your mercy, grace, and love to share with others. Help us to be living epistles of Jesus Christ. In Your name, we pray, amen.

October 10

Happy are those whose trust is in the Lord. Mountains may crumble, the earth may shake, but we will not be overcome.

He has given His word that He support all who trust in Him. Sometimes that means walking through the most challenging part of life by faith alone, with our eyes on the Father.

As I write this, I can't help but recall my own dear dad. At the end of his time on this earth, I remember the peace I felt amid the chaos. Yes, the world that I knew was being shaken. But the peace of God that passes all human understanding surrounded us as we witnessed our father being ushered home.

For some time afterward, people would say to me, "Your dad's viewing and service were beautiful." I know it sounds odd, but God can make the hardest time of your life serene as you place yourself in His ever-loving arms.

October 11

One day at 4:55 p.m., I was getting ready to leave work. Just then my boss sent me an email asking me to check a report status that had been pending. That meant making a phone call, which would take a few minutes. I felt annoyed that he'd asked me to do this right before punching out. But of course I made the call.

Soon enough I jumped in my car and proceeded home via the usual route. Halfway down the first stretch of road, I saw flashing lights, and as I got closer, I saw two cars that had just been involved in a horrible collision. By the looks of the scene, it seemed that the accident occurred within the last five minutes.

At that second a chill ran through me as I thought that I could have very well been involved in that accident, had I not been detained at work. I thanked God for unexpected, last-minute "inconveniences" in my schedule. God is always on time when we need Him most.

October 12

This is a story about Gigi, my cat. I got her over 4 years ago from a private owner. Gigi came out of an abusive situation—not by the hands of people, but rather animals. Gigi was being picked on, bullied, and beat up by other cats in the household. She took to hiding in a cubby hole for months. Food was daily placed there. But when she was finally lured out, she was skin and bones and full of scabs from wounds inflicted by the other cats.

She was finally placed in another room where the offenders could not get to her. But the damage to her psyche had already been done. Even now, sometimes I'll go to pet her, and I see a look of terror in her eyes for a moment.

And I wonder how many people are like Gigi. They have been wounded by abuse, rejection, isolation, or separation, and they are afraid to truly trust and love again. Only God can heal such wounds and make someone whole.

I always say that I am not a cat person and Gigi is not a person cat. But because of love, we make it work. Maybe you have been wounded in life, or you know someone who has. God will bring people together who understand brokenness and work to restore them, through His power and love.

October 13

Was I not young just yesterday? Living life is proof that it is merely a breath.

When I was young, I used to believe that I had all the time in the world. I would think, *I'll get with Jesus tomorrow.*

Then "tomorrow" turns into months and years.

One of our enemy's main strategies used against us is the desire to delay.

So, before we begin our day, let us start the morning by giving back to the Lord. He has saved us from the pit of destruction. Let us show gratitude for a life eternal.

Lord, We love You and we want to thank You for saving us. Your gift of life eternal is worthy of our praise. I give You my life. Help me to live purposefully for You. In Jesus's name, amen.

October 14

I realized something about me.
I was living in a lack of vitality.
The truth be known,
I loved my God,
But my passion died.
When did it go?
I am in a state of awareness now.
I asked the Father, "Show me how!"
I prayed a desperate, wanting prayer.
I begged, "Jesus, take me there!
Give me the hunger to want more of You,
To share more of Your saving truth.
Help me abandon worldly desires,
Set this heart for You on fire."
Suddenly it all is changed,
Nothing will ever be the same.
The vision's clear,
My eyes see now,
The day draws near,
When every knee will bow.
His marching orders,
"Go now! Be on your path and show all,
By carrying the news I bring.
My name is Love and I am King!
Come to Me; you will never thirst,
I am the living reservoir!
My life is eternally yours,
I am the Christ of open doors."

October 15

When God says forever, He means it! Forget the other wishy-washy half promises you've heard throughout your life. Don't go there by getting into comparisons. He is the ultimate promise keeper.

Can you say "infinity"? That is the amount of time He will be on your side. In other words, He is never, ever gonna give up on you!

Though your heart has sustained major damage, trust the healer. His MO is LOVE! Ultimate, perfect, and true!

Hand it all over to Him and He will write your destiny and keep you in His heart forever!

October 16

Our attitude of obedience should never stop!

While taking my morning stop for tea at the local coffee shop, I approached the drive-thru. A man in a very large truck sped in front of me.

How rude! was my first thought, but I heard the Lord say, *"Let it go."* So I did not entertain that idea one second longer. I said, "Thanks for the advice, Lord."

When God talks to me, I try to always obey and thank Him for His guidance. I am grateful that I have a Father, friend, advocate, and teacher to walk me through Life 101. It's the still, small voice that lives on the inside, which we need to be acutely aware of, lest we silence it with our mortality. He will speak, if we listen.

Incidentally, when I got to the drive-thru window, the cashier said, "The car in front of you was the owner. He paid for your order."

Obedience: yielding to the one who knows all. Lesson learned!

October 17

It's time to shine! Just as Esther of the Bible was born "for such a time as this" (Esther 4:14 NKJV), I believe we have also been born at a pivotal time to make a difference in the world.

If we choose, we can change our world. It doesn't matter how big or small we may consider ourselves, God will use our gifts and talents in some way. If you are willing, He will make you able!

Perhaps today is the moment for which you have been created!

October 18

God has got this. Don't worry!

I know you've been enduring for a long time. But wait until you see what He has for you!

Keep putting one foot in front of the other. Even if you don't feel like it's working, just do it anyway!

I know that the struggle is real some days! But God is far greater than the challenge. Do not look at the size of the obstacle in your path. Keep your sights on the miraculous. No matter how deep and dark the pit you find yourself in, He will always pull you out!

God, You are power, You are love! I know You will bring ultimate victory to my situation. I believe and receive it in Jesus's name, amen.

October 19

Keep the faith! I know there are times when we feel like giving up. But when all seems hopeless, remember this: God is not through with you yet.

There are many opportunities to become frustrated. We sometimes allow ourselves to be led by our emotions. However, God's ways are not governed by the way we feel. If we believe in our hearts, regardless of what our minds dwell on, breakthrough will come!

It might have been days, weeks, years—but God's not a quitter. His ways are higher than our ways. He sees the overall greater outcome and He will not stop until it's done. He may have you change direction and go a completely different route. But you can be assured, if you listen to His voice, the vision will come to fruition. God is faithful!

October 20

There's a peace I've come to know—no matter what tempests may come across life's path. It is a calm above the storm. It is hope beyond the circumstances.

He is the Truth. He is peace. God is astounding in how He infiltrates the cloud of reasoning and judgment, and illuminates our spirit.

When the calamity and chaos of existence try to serve a heaping helping of oppression upon you, just say "Jesus!"

He will come, He will calm, He will conquer!

What liberty to us who had been in shackles, left battered and bruised by the attacks! We are former slaves. But now we stand, liberated. The Judge has slammed the gavel. With one swift swoop, the verdict is in: We are forgiven!

It is well with my soul. It is well.

October 21

Love is an action word.

It never expires or quits trying. It builds up. It soothes and
heals.

It is silent when the urge to be angry rises up.

It speaks words of comfort in due season.

It makes allowances for misunderstandings and pardons the
unforgivable.

It shares the burden when one alone cannot handle the load.

It gives without notice of reciprocation.

Love will not exist without the willingness to share it.

Let us every day aspire to be philanthropists of love.

October 22

The love that bound Jesus to the cross is the very same love that is "shed abroad" in our hearts today (Romans 5:5 KJV).

Sometimes that love is not an easy love. Faithful love can be tough, after all. It can be gut wrenching to watch someone you love endure pain. Yet those are the ties that bind.

Enduring our own desert seasons has the potential to make us hard-hearted and bitter. But the very challenging times can also cause our love to grow deeper and stronger. Though we yearn for some respite from the hardships of life, our hearts can mature if we allow ourselves to grow better and not bitter.

Do not harden your hearts when challenges come. Ask the Lord, "What can I learn from this?" And then grow in the love and knowledge that God would desire for you.

With God's help, every day, in every way, we are getting better!

October 23

Being an animal lover, I have watched dozens of rescues recorded on video.

There is one common denominator with all the animals that are being rescued: Unless the animal is incapacitated by either sickness or injury, they are sure to flee from the rescuers.

They fear people because of some prior abuse, they have come to think of man as their enemy.

But once they are caught, they usually collapse in the rescuer's arms and surrender themselves wholeheartedly.

People who elude God are a lot like these creatures.

Although God has wonderful plans for us, most people, like the animals will run in fear because of some preconceived notions about His intentions.

Just as an animal is vulnerable, and in danger from predators and the elements outside, people are susceptible to countless attacks from the devil without Jesus.

At the moment we finally surrender to God, we can rest assured that we are at last safe and sound in our beloved Savior's arms. We are indeed rescued.

October 24

Who do you think you are? A lot of people on this big round ball we call "earth" do not have a very high opinion of themselves. Some may think it's okay—"At least I'm not proud and arrogant, right?" they may say.

Not true! Although God does not want us to be arrogant, His desire is for us to believe the best about ourselves. As our Creator, He sees our potential, our good side, our unique qualities. He doesn't look at us and say, "What a disappointment you are! You're a loser."

Yet many of us hear these words echo in our minds again and again. Maybe the words originated with family, friends, or peers. Perhaps it was our own thoughts as we gazed at our reflection in the mirror.

No matter how it started, words become thoughts, become reasoning, become mind-sets. It's an ugly trap set by the enemy of our souls to hinder our godly potential. But in reality, we are brilliant stars on God's heavenly "walk of fame."

His love has the potential to send our self-esteem soaring because He is crazy about you and me. So remember: it's not who you are, but whose you are. You are a child of the King—and God does not make junk!

October 25

There are 366 scriptures on "do not fear" in the Bible—one for every day of the year, including an extra day for leap year. Wow! What foresight our Lord has to know that we would need instructions for dealing with fear so often.

We have so many opportunities to experience fear. But that does not mean we have to let fear consume us. When you are feeling challenged to do something that you know you have do, just open the Bible and refer to a "do not fear" scripture to empower you to push through.

Joyce Meyer offered some wise words to use in such times: "Giving in to fear alters God's best plan for your life. So use the power of God's Word to do what He wants you to do—even if you have to do it afraid!"

October 26

How I admire those who sacrifice the comfort and safety of their homes to go on a missions trip. Years ago I said to God, "How I wish I could be so brave as to go on the missions field." The Lord then showed me that we can all be "mobile missionaries" by spreading God's message of love and caring to those right in our own backyards.

We do not have to go across the world to give of our time, our money, and our love. God gives us many opportunities to reach out and touch others. We just need to open our eyes. Whether it be in a supermarket, at work, or on the street, a smile or a kind word can be just what someone needs to get through their day.

Let us seize every occasion to be givers of hope and love to the downcast. That is a mission we can make possible!

October 27

One night the power went off. I sat in the dark for a couple hours and reflected on how we take the light for granted. Likewise, we always assume God is there … and it's true that He is.

But what about people who live in this godless world without any sense of knowing the Lord of the universe. In a spiritual sense they are living in a blackened haze of hopelessness, not realizing they can access a beautiful light and never be in the dark again.

Lord, we pray for those alone and lost without You. Bring them to the one true light that is Yours.

In Jesus's name.

October 28

Seeking His face,

Loving God's grace,

He knows my life story.

Yet He doesn't ignore me.

Sin has set me back,

Another attack,

Evil's lurking,

My Savior's working,

Another day, another prayer,

God, help me, I'm here!

I am not worthy,

Again Jesus heard me.

Delivered me, rescued from the mud,

Set on the rock,

Because of the blood!

His heart, it beats,

His eyes that weep,

The words He speaks,

The soul He seeks,

The needs He meets!

Give Him all the glory,

For rewriting our story.

October 29

It often begins with a feeling, an impression. To further dwell upon such an impression then open the door to the enemy's whispers. The tension mounts within us, and soon, very soon, the whispers become shouts in our heads: "Don't let them get away with that!" or "They are making a fool out of you!" or "You deserve better!"

Who is it that generates the dark voices streaming daily against our minds? He is the insidious master behind every offensive thought we feel. He wreaks havoc every place he goes. He provides the filthy grease to keep the wheel of dissent turning. But we give him a legal permit by taking the bait.

When evil knocks on the door, just say, "Jesus, can You get that?" Tell that devil to take a hike down the road. We can reverse the curse by not buying the lies. Jesus is the enemy's kryptonite! He will keep our fleshly thoughts from becoming words and actions that turn into regrets.

October 30

Recently I was pouring water from a pitcher and suddenly realized how we take this for granted. If it were not for gravity, this simple action would be impossible. But because this has been tested and tried, we think nothing of it.

Regardless of the advances of modern technology, gravity remains a wonder of science. Yet who created gravity? How can one have faith in the invention and not have faith in the inventor?

Many believe in the logic of science, but do not believe in the existence of our Creator. They want to see God to believe in Him. Yet gravity cannot be seen. Air cannot be seen. People know gravity and air are real because we could not exist on earth without either one.

As for God, His way is perfect! The word of the Lord is tested and tried; He is a shield to all those who take refuge and put their trust in Him.
Psalm 18:30 (AMPCE)

Every word of God is tried and purified.
Proverbs 30:5 (AMPCE)

For in Him we live and move and have our being....
Acts 17:28 (AMPCE)

I know that His awesome power is beyond our comprehension and inconceivable to the human mind. He is real. He is God!

October 31

He touched me one day. When once I was lost in sin, when I had no notion of following God, He gave it all for me!

I wandered aimlessly, as one who had no home. I did not know my heart was secretly crying out. And He heard me. He pulled me out of the muck and the mire— placed me on solid ground.

The promise is for everyone. If you believe there is a clause that makes you exempt, you are incorrect. Jesus is for the underdogs who have slipped between the cracks of this life.

If you are hiding, He will find you and make a believer out of you. Bring it all and spare nothing. Just lay it down! He can handle it!

Give God a chance to fix you for real!

November 1

Jesus came to save the spiritually lost. But His aspirations for us do not stop there. He wants us to thrive, not just survive.

He wants you to comprehend His redemption is the full package. It contains all the bells and whistles. And don't compare it to car shopping: you know what you want, but you get what you can afford. In other words forget the sunroof, heated seats, and stereo. It's out of the realm of possibility for you. So you settle for manual locks, AM radio, and windows you have to crank open.

Jesus Christ isn't like that! He came so we may have abundant life, according to John 10:10. *Strong's Concordance* says that this abundant life means "full to the overflow, more than enough, excessive, lavish."

God's desire is for us to live in fullness every day so that we can give life away! I am not only speaking spiritually, but also emotionally, physically, and financially.

How can we help others when we are barely getting along ourselves? The notion that God wants to keep us down and out is not biblical. He wants to bring fullness to our lives so that we in turn can reciprocate by giving to others and speaking of God's goodness.

He came so that we may have life more abundantly!

November 2

God is covering His earth with a blanket of His love. He stands at every point and echoes words of life, setting forth growth, provision, and abundance.

See His works in the everyday things He is bringing to pass: the green grass, the leaves on the trees, the flowers, all showing their marvelous colors; He gives us "rainbows" every day—promises of a something new ... new creations to behold.

As long as we look with our spiritual eyes wide open, we will witness His glory, His splendor, His majesty. Everywhere, we will see His face.

I had heard of you [only] by the hearing of the ear, but now my [spiritual] eye sees You.
Job 42:5 (AMPCE)

November 3

I know that no matter what hardship comes my way in this life, God is good all the time! I believe that while there is much suffering in the world, He is always faithful.

Temptation came. Man fell. Sin entered the world. God's Eden was pure perfection. But man made a choice to take the dark road. Evil is why bad things happen to good people.

First Peter 5:8 (NIV) tells us: "Be alert and of sober mind. Your enemy the devil prowls around like a roaring lion looking for someone to devour." He lurks about, positioning himself for an opportunity to kill, steal, and destroy, but all the while, Jesus offers life more abundantly (John 10:10).

Even as evil waits for an opportunity to attack, Jesus stands by, waiting for us to call His name. "Do not wallow in your suffering," He says to us. "Just call out My name and praise Me, and the enemy will have to flee."

Yes, we live in a fallen, sinful world. But we have a choice about whom we give place to in our lives. The power of Jesus far supersedes the enemy's power over us— if we give God the authority over our lives. Remember always what 1 John 4:4 (NIV) says: "You, dear children, are from God and have overcome them, because the one who is in you is greater than the one who is in the world."

November 4

Quiet as the morning dew,

The sunlight creeps into my room.

Waking with God's loving thoughts,

My day is starting soon.

It is the moment to go and reach within

To the garden of my soul,

To touch the inner springs of life,

Through Him I know I'm whole.

It's time to hear the message

That in silence speaks,

To feast, His living manna,

My inner spirit seeks.

It is a place of silence,

A golden, sacred hour.

Where Spirit speaks to spirit's own,

God touches with His power.

November 5

Recently on a Christian radio station, I heard the testimony of a mother and father whose baby was diagnosed at birth with a form of mitochondrial disease, which would be a terminal condition. The doctors told the parents their son would not live past two years. So the parents decided they would cherish every moment they would have with their precious baby.

One day they were in the store and the baby reached out and grabbed a greeting card off the shelf. The dad went to put the card back, but he stopped when he noticed these words on the front of the card: "Behold, I will bring to it health and healing, and I will heal them and reveal to them abundance of prosperity and security" (Jeremiah 33:6 ESV). The father was amazed and purchased the card.

When they arrived home, the father found a package in the mail, from a ministry, and he opened it. Inside the package was a card that read: *Jeremiah 33:6—* *"Behold, I will bring to it health and healing, and I will heal them and reveal to them abundance of prosperity and security."*

After this day the medical team caring for the baby found no evidence of mitochondrial disease in his body.

I am here to encourage you in the fact that we serve a miracle-working God who loves to bring hope to the hopeless!

November 6

I had been seeing the same man on the same corner for quite some time. God had placed it upon my heart a while ago to offer him money. This guy was not begging, but every time I passed him, I felt a tugging in my heart to help him. I thought of a hundred excuses why I shouldn't assist him. But I only had one reason to help him, which became the definitive answer: because He said so!

Remember when you were little and you questioned why you had to do something, and your mom or dad answered, "Because I said so!" We dared not argue the point beyond those words. This was the message I got from God, and that was why I finally stopped one morning to be obedient to the Lord's request.

I got out of my car and the man said, "Hello there!"

I replied, "I thought you could use this to get some breakfast. God bless you."

"Uh-huh, yep," he said.

I guess I felt hesitant because I didn't want to insult the guy. But after exchanging words with him, I realized he was mentally challenged and was not at all put out by my offering.

I have to tell you how much better I felt after I got back in my car. It wasn't a "pat myself on the back" feeling." It was like God smiled and said, *"Now that wasn't so hard, was it?"*

I just smiled and answered, "No, Lord, it wasn't."

November 7

If you are feeling like you are at the end of your rope, tie a knot and hold on! God is right there beside you, helping you to get through this thing called life.

Yes, there will be days when every moment seems like an eternity and forging ahead feels like an impossibility. I cannot tell you the number of times I've felt this way. Sometimes I yielded myself to God and allowed Him to carry me every step of the way. Yet other times I just felt I had to do it my way. Let me tell you: standing in God's way never works. He will let you do your own thing, sure. But, boy, are you going to be sorry and sore!

The following is a humorous poem I wrote that illustrates what happens when we do things our way:

> "Lord, in the 'Footprints' poem, there's one set in
>   the sand,
> Mine are quite different, you see?
> Beside Your prints, there are two lines,
> What could this possibly be?"
> And Jesus replied, "It simply means, as I carried
>   you through, you were dragging your feet."

November 8

Jesus Christ taught me how to hope. Prior to knowing Him, I could not experience hope. Continual disappointment breaks the bough of the thoughts of a better tomorrow. Soon, learning to expect the worst becomes the norm.

Then, when a favorable outcome occurs, the hopeless will believe it only to be a "cosmic happenstance," not that someone is looking out for our greater good. That's where I found myself—but then I met Jesus.

Everything changed. I no longer placed my trust in the odds of my universe, which was a crapshoot at best. I placed my hope in the reliable hands of the One who gave His all for me. He brought me up from the miry clay of life and set my feet upon the rock of His salvation. In loving me, Jesus caused me to trust, hope, and have faith.

I no longer wake up and roll the dice. I give it all over to the King of kings. He navigates and steers the course of my life with brilliant precision. I may wander off from time to time, but I always return home—to Him.

On Christ alone, the Rock, I'll stand. All other ground is shifting sand.

November 9

Be a wave maker! Be a promoter for all that is good and fair in this world. The opposition is staggering, yes! But let it be known that we will not go placidly into the night. We will resist the evil that persistently aims to take over our existence.

Many will surrender to the majority and sacrifice their beliefs to silence. However, I will ride the wave of faith in my God until the tide turns. Or I will die trying.

Evil persists, but God will prevail! Many will call it obstinacy. But we will face the lies and be lions for the truth. Although we are of the few, we are not alone. The battle ensues in the heavens on our behalf.

No matter how things appear. We will win the fight. God will not concede. He has the final word.

November 10

Love like there's no tomorrow. Be that person who makes a difference. Someone is out there in the world, feeling as if no one cares. While you are going about your day, let the person before, behind, or beside you know that they matter.

If you are stuck in traffic, start a wave of waves. Buy coffee for the next car in the drive-thru.

Everyone is fighting a battle. We never know what anyone is going through—unless we care enough to inquire. Go the extra mile and ask, "Can I help you?"

It doesn't cost anything to love. But the dividends are enormous.

We can make a difference in this world, one kind act at a time. Let us be the example to others to go above and beyond the daily requirements.

Be a life giver, a do-gooder, an ambassador of love. Today make someone smile.

November 11

How can I visit the stars,

While I am stuck in the clouds?

I reach for new heights, but they seem to liquefy in my grasp.

Bring it on! I boldly proclaim.

Then I shrink and cower, feeling insignificant and small in my reality.

The voice of my nemesis is merely an echo of my own negative thinking.

I sink deeper still into a cavernous region of past failures.

But out of the depths of my heart,

An anchor of hope is cast.

"Catch it. Here it comes." You say.

"It is my Love and it rises above all the darkness.

Hold onto it with all your might and never let it go.

You are meant for so much more than you can imagine.

Believe for big miracles!"

November 12

I am on a road of restoration.

I've opted to allow the Master to perform open heart surgery on me.

It is a painful process, for certain!

But my desire is to be healed the right way.

I am weary of trying in my own strength. Just when I believe I am doing better, my heart sustains another bruise. The pain cuts deep and I feel the wound may be fatal.

"Toughen up!" My Mother used to say when I felt hurt by people's actions. She just didn't want me to be hurt anymore.

But I do not want to be tough, I want to be strong.

Being tough denotes a form of callousness, a hardness if you will.

Building strength through God will enable us to handle the hurts, without becoming hard-hearted.

I cannot say I will never let myself to be hurt again.

But I will continue to allow God in to restore, when I am in need of healing.

November 13

A "psalm" is defined as "a sacred song or poem used in worship." In the Bible the book of Psalms was authored by several people. But, of the 150 chapters in Psalms, David is named as the author of 73. David was also called "a man after [God's] own heart" (1 Samuel 13:14 NKJV).

In spite of David's faults, his ups and downs, his many sins against God, God truly loved David. Why? Perhaps it was David's true love for God and his humility. David possessed the ability to see his sins and quickly repent. Most of all, David loved God with all of his heart, he depended solely upon Him, and he lived to worship Him. God loved David's heart.

Oh, if we could only be more like David—to have a deep desire to pray to the Father, to praise Him, and to pour our hearts out to Him, just as David did in the psalms he penned.

God loves all His children with an unending love. God does not recognize a religion; He only desires a true relationship with Him through Jesus Christ His Son. God focuses on our heart condition. He responds to our prayers when we ask in sincerity and love.

The earnest (heartfelt, continued) prayer of a righteous man makes tremendous power available [dynamic in its working].
James 5:16 (AMPCE)

November 14

Why does it seem as though ungodly people always seem to get ahead? Maybe you have always tried to do the right thing. Yet all of your life you have struggled to make it—even as you watch those who are dishonest seem to come out smelling like a rose.

The Bible states: "Never envy the wicked! Soon they fade away like grass and disappear. Trust in the Lord instead. Be kind and good to others; then you will live safely here in the land and prosper, feeding in safety" (Psalm 37:1–3 TLB).

So let us not focus on our misfortunes, but on our many blessings. Dwelling on what others have will only create resentment. We begin to ask questions like, "Why them? Why not me?"

Bitterness is a trail that the enemy uses to derail our Christian walk. Many have gone down the "poor me" trail, only to experience negative results.

Many times the greedy prosper with regard to material wealth. But nothing can compare to the priceless gift of Jesus Christ.

Do not lay up for yourselves treasures on earth,
where moth and rust destroy and where thieves break in
and steal, but lay up for yourselves treasures in heaven,
where neither moth nor rust destroys and where thieves do
not break in and steal. For where your treasure is, there
your heart will be also.
Matthew 6:19–21 (ESV)

November 15

Give, and it will be given to you: good measure, pressed
down, shaken together, and running over will be put into
your bosom. For with the same measure that you use, it will
be measured back to you.
Luke 6:38 (NKJV)

I heartily subscribe to God's view of giving. God does not
want us to give to take from us. On the contrary, the
concept of reciprocity centers on how our giving will be
returned to us—multiplied.

Case in point: Until recently, I had financially
supported a Christian radio station. When I lost my full-
time job, I stopped giving to the station.

Not long afterward, the station was running a
pledge drive. While I was driving and tuned in to the
station, the thought burned inside me that I should renew
my pledge. But I dismissed the thought.

Almost at once I noticed that the car in front of me
had a license plate that read "REDEEMD"—for
"redeemed," I thought it a bit unusual to see such a plate,
but then that car turned the corner and the vehicle now in
front of me had a plate that read: "PLEDGE."

Wow! I could hardly believe my eyes!

As soon as I arrived home, I phoned the station and
renewed my pledge.

One day later on when I was feeling anxious about
having enough money, God said to me, *"Your God will*
supply all your needs—not your job!"

November 16

God knows what He is doing! Even though we may not be aware of what is going on behind the scenes, so to speak, God has a strategic plan for our lives.

It may look to us like we're just spinning our wheels. But God is tirelessly proactive in fulfilling a vision.

Case in point: I had been asking God for a new job for more than two years. I would say, "Lord, I do not believe this is where You want me to stay."

Struggling and striving, I finally reconciled within myself that God is the designer of my destiny.

Shortly after, I got the opportunity to live in a place with almost no overhead, and God landed me a job that would be rewarding and beneficial to others. In retrospect I can see why it hadn't happened sooner. The new job would mean taking a cut in pay, and it wouldn't have been feasible where I had been living. But obtaining the new place to live took the strain off my finances, and therefore I was able to take the plunge with the new lower-paying job.

Always believe God is working with your best interests at heart. As Jesus professed in His Holy Word, even unto the cross: "Nevertheless, not my will, but yours, be done" (Luke 22:42 ESV).

God is in control!

November 17

The human tendency is to fill the ominous void inside us with "stuff" so we do not feel empty. We believe that occupying our lives with drugs, food, alcohol, sex, or material things will free us from the gnawing sensation that lingers inside. If anything, it's a temporary fix. But soon after, the void has returned with a vengeance to make our lives unlivable.

So how do we fix what is broken inside us? We can't. But Jesus can!

He is the master of mending. The repairer of the breach. The restorer of streets to dwell upon. He is the great shepherd to His sheep, and the potter to His clay. He loves us with an everlasting love and that doesn't go away!

When life has shattered your hopes and dreams, don't just try to fill the void. Look to the One who will create beauty from our ashes. Look to the One who will never leave you or forsake you. Trust Jesus to make you smile again.

November 18

This is from a loving Father who loves you far beyond what the world has to offer.

He calls to you with a soft beckoning voice,

Come and sit with Me awhile.

Though men can hurt you,

do not believe this to be a reflection of My feelings for you.

You are my beloved daughter and I cherish you.

I knitted you together in your Mother's womb.

Stop searching and wandering about, as a child with no direction.

I have great plans for you, not for destruction.

Yet the enemy of everyone's souls,

will do just that if you take that road.

You are whom you named your first born son,

You are a Christian,

Now resume your life as one.

November 19

You've given all you could. Now it's time to give again!

Your inner resources have been exhausted. You wait for the refreshing. But it doesn't arrive. You're feeling tapped out. Another day, another challenge, presents itself.

I am not referring to monetary expenditures—but that can definitely apply also. Today I am addressing the topic of emotional and spiritual bankruptcy.

The dreams that lay dormant—the "hope deferred" (Proverbs 13:12 NIV)—may become despair as we are attacked yet again. However intense the struggle, though, will be equivalent to the glory at breakthrough—if we do not lose heart, friends!

Prayerfully proceed until He positively provides the promise. Jesus will outlast every evil that aims to beset your dreams. And the best part is, you will come out even stronger.

Victory is imminent through Christ Jesus!

November 20

You are testing the waters. You're waiting for the ultimate litmus test to find the truth. Just maybe your faith has grown old, or cold. The Word just doesn't excite you like it used to.

Will waiting ever convince us that God is really real? Let me put this theory to rest now. The answer is definitively "No!"

I recall the seasons of my life when I said, "I'll just see if God parts the waters," and I can assure you it's a trap. The word "trap" in the New Testament comes from the Greek word *skandalon*: "a stick for bait (of a trap), a stumbling block, an offense."

Delay is the oldest trick that comes from the enemy. You will hear these kinds of words echo in your mind: *"You're too tired to read the Bible"*—and your eyes will grow heavier.

Do not wait for the perfect time, my friends!

It's simple really. Let me offer you a starting point: "Jesus, I confess I am a sinner. I believe You died on the cross to save me. I ask You to come into my heart and make It Your home. Amen."

If you have prayed that prayer more than once, it's okay. So have I.

God gives us a million opportunities to accept His invitation. But we only have one reason why we don't accept: we wait.

Don't wait until it's too late!

November 21

In the darkest night, the smallest prayer will ignite a light to see you through to morning. The shadows are ominous. But God is the shadow chaser, and He will seek you out.

No fears, nor tears, will scare Him away. He has seen it all before: the good, the bad, and the ugly. Yet He believes you are worth hanging around for.

Your sins, no matter how many, are a thing of the past, when you surrender it all to Him. I'm talking about a clean slate! Look at what the Father promises to us in Isaiah 1:18 (NIV): "'Come now, let us settle the matter,' says the LORD. 'Though your sins are like scarlet, they shall be as white as snow; though they are red as crimson, they shall be like wool.'"

He has been there, and He will remain. When you are in pain and you feel like you are doing life alone, Jesus is there.

The heartache is real. But He is more real—and steadfast until the end. He won't leave you in the lurch like others have. No, on the contrary, He will put you on a pedestal. He will cause your light to shine for all to see.

And if you lose your way again, do not be afraid to come home. He is waiting, with arms open wide.

November 22

The huge droplets of rain pelted my car, ferocious thunder rumbled overhead. It was challenging to drive, as my windshield wipers couldn't overcome the torrential downpour.

At a red light, I sat there, transfixed on the dark clouds looming over our great city. Suddenly I saw a flock of geese flying high above. It then occurred to me that, in spite of the heavy rain, they persevered. The showers did not deter them from the goal of reaching their destination.

Shortly after, as I reached the foot of a hill, I saw a man zoom by on a motorcycle. *How curious,* I thought. *A motorcycle ride in the rain.* I watched as the guy pressed on in spite of the downpour.

Do you not see there is a wonderful lesson in this?

Into one's life, rain will certainly fall. It is what we do with our rainy days that will ultimately determine our altitude in life. We can either wait for the rain to cease, or we can choose to soar through the clouds to reach great heights—or ride on through the rain, embracing every moment we have as a gift from our Father.

As one famous quotation puts it: "Life isn't about waiting for the storm to pass. It's about learning to dance in the rain."

November 23

We aspire for godliness and goodness to be the new norm. We crave peace, but not as the world gives—rather, a real taste of tranquility breaking through the heaviness of civilization.

As we know, though, we will not experience true *shalom*—peace and wholeness—until we are ushered to our heavenly home. The Bible states, "If you belonged to the world, it would love you as its own. As it is, you do not belong to the world, but I have chosen you out of the world. That is why the world hates you" (John 15:19 NIV).

As they hated Jesus, they will also hate us. Nevertheless we can cheerfully accept our lot in life. All the opposition, the turmoil, the resistance, should not sway our position.

Yes, we yearn for a world without all the calamity and chaos. But it cannot be, so long as sin abides on the planet. So we will continue to march to the beat of a minority, and pledge to yield to our heavenly Father—our Lord, the one true God, whose grave stands vacant, while the graves of others who claimed to be gods are still inhabited by their remains.

Yes, the tomb is empty. Yet our hearts are filled with His presence. And though we cannot achieve true "world peace" until the day Jesus returns, we can have peace within us—when He is in us.

November 24

Remember those times you'd come in from playing outside all day as a child? So often, after a long day of playing outdoors, I was dirty from head to toe. As I walked through the door, my mom would occasionally announce, "You look like a ragamuffin!" I did not know what a "ragamuffin" was then, but I knew it wasn't a good thing.

Many of us wander through life feeling like ragamuffins. Somehow, because of the opinions of others, or our own, we have deemed ourselves unfit.

Maybe you have concluded that your nose, or your lips, or your entire body is too large, or perhaps you feel ugly, inside or out. It does not matter. Rejection of self steals your happiness, and ultimately your life.

Satan's goal is to take your salvation. If he cannot do that, he will attempt to apprehend your self-esteem, your dreams, your life force. If he can't get you to hell, he will attempt to bring you hell on earth.

The Bible says, "For you created my inmost being; you knit me together in my mother's womb. I praise you because I am fearfully and wonderfully made; your works are wonderful, I know that full well" (Psalm 139:13–14 NIV).

No matter what thoughts enter our minds, we do not have to entertain or accept them. When the world rejects you, make a choice to accept God's opinion over everyone else's. If you are feeling less than perfect, remember that the King of the universe is so in love with you!

November 25

Talk to Me, and I will share secrets that you've never known.

I will tell you how I reached out and scattered the stars, dispersing and naming each and every one.

I have grafted each snowflake to outshine any masterpiece the greatest artist can depict.

I am the master builder. With time, I have set the majestic mountains, and created valleys of crimson and gray.

I have aligned the oceans with perfect precision and have filled the vastness of them with treasures to behold.

I have given you the trees of the forest, every size and shape, and created animals of every species to inhabit them.
All life is in My grasp.
Then, there is My greatest creation. You!
I made you in my image and likeness.
I took the rib from a man and created woman. I said, man should not be alone.
I created love and when sin entered and man had fallen, I created Hope.
Through that Hope is life eternal.
No man can come to Me, but through Him.
Witness the wonder of Jesus Christ today.

November 26

Just take it off! Remove the weighty encumbrances of the guilt that previously entrapped you. Take hold of the keys of emancipation, and live fully with Jesus! Remember always what God promised in Isaiah 1:17 (NIV): "'Come now, let us settle the matter,' says the LORD. 'Though your sins are like scarlet, they shall be as white as snow; though they are red as crimson, they shall be like wool.'"

So it begins. Take heed no more to the voices that plague you with condemnation. It is God Himself who has granted your liberty. The proclamation was delivered the day He stretched Himself out on the cross and declared we are worth dying for.

Gone are the days of dashed hopes and dreams. Jesus is your new hope for a better tomorrow. No more shall we run the gauntlet of the oppressed., but we will grab the baton to run our race with enthusiasm.

No matter how many times we fall, we will rise again. We are assured of a victorious outcome. Let our hearts be glad and our anthem remain, "In all these things we are more than conquerors through him who loved us" (Romans 8:37).

November 27

Live life large on purpose!

Keep in mind Habakkuk 2:3 (KJV): "For the vision is yet for an appointed time, but at the end it shall speak, and not lie: though it tarry, wait for it; because it will surely come, it will not tarry." Wait for it! But only stay still and wait *after* you had used all of your resources to help make the dream come to pass.

Never settle for ordinary. You were made for much more than that. The other guy might be okay with "just getting by." But that is not you. You can feel it in your bones. You've never fit in—never blended in.

Now it is time to show your polka dots with pinstripe attributes, and make God proud. You see, He loves all who the world may call "foolish." He uses the quirky ones to get things done.

And it is in the final round that you will know it was all worth it. With every fiber of your being exhausted from the task, your spirit will be soaring and your heart full. You will finally hear the words, "Well done, good and faithful servant." Then you will know: you've done good.

November 28

The topic for today brings to mind a popular 70s song entitled, "How Can You Mend A Broken Heart."

The idea that a heart could physically be broken seems nonsensical and beyond logic. However, recent research recognizes a malady called "broken heart syndrome" as a legitimate condition. Studies of thousands of cases show individuals, while in a devastating situation, suffered heart-related problems.

Whether it's heart disease, heart failure, or atrial fibrillation, it appears tragedies can literally cause heartbreak. We have heard cases of someone dying, then shortly after the spouse also dies. It seems the human heart is so closely linked to the emotions, that they are one and the same.

In Proverbs 27:19 (), we see this truth echoed in the words, "As water reflects the face,
so one's life reflects the heart."

In another verse from Proverbs, the Lord offers us advice on how we can help strengthen our hearts: "Guard your heart above all else, for it determines the course of your life" (4:23 NLT).

Ultimately our choice should be to place our hearts in the capable hands of the One who created it!

November 29

I have a friend who raises doves. He recently built a new enclosure, because the old one had fallen into disrepair. It became a challenge to transfer the birds into the new cage.

Five doves escaped in the process, and they kept returning to the old location of the former enclosure. Little did they know that a bigger, better place awaited them. Ultimately my friend caught four, and only one dove remained on the loose. My friend made several attempts to rescue the lone dove. Finally, the bird found its way to the new housing, but every time someone drew close, it escaped.

The bird grew weary as the weeks passed. It had to seek shelter, find food, and escape predators. At long last, my friend rescued the dove.

How exhausting! It occurred to me, the same could be said about existence without God. Even as He offers us a new life, people will often gravitate back to familiar surroundings. His plan is to offer us sanctuary from the predators of the world, and to provide sustenance for our lives. But so often, to our detriment, the choice is made to escape God's embrace and brave it alone.

The Bible states, "where the spirit of the Lord is, there is liberty" (2 Corinthians 3:17 NKJV). So in order to experience true emancipation from the entrapments of the world, we need to understand His way is best.

November 30

*The Lord is my shepherd; I shall not want. He maketh me
to lie down in green pastures: he leadeth me beside the still
waters. He restoreth my soul: he leadeth me in the paths of
righteousness for his name's sake. Yea, though I walk
through the valley of the shadow of death, I will fear no
evil: for thou art with me; thy rod and thy staff they comfort
me.*
Psalm 23: 1–4 (KJV)

We often hear Psalm 23 from the Bible being read when
someone is very ill, or has passed on from this life to the
next. However, I believe these verses are ones of hope and
faith.

As we study the words, we can observe that the
writer affirms the Lord is a guiding force and He will not
leave us wanting. If we trust in Him, we can rest assured
He is watching over us. He transforms our soul and delivers
us unto righteousness through His holy name. In spite of
tragedy, we will not fear. The Lord is always with us. His
shepherd's rod and staff help to lead, guide, and train us to
walk in His way and abide in His Word.

We have the ultimate promise of His presence and
protection, as well as eternal life, when we follow God's
path for us.

December 1

With December here again and Christmas not far away, it won't be long before many of us go out to get a tree for our homes. A few years ago I discovered a fact that gave the evergreen tree new meaning for me.

Someone had told me at springtime (around Easter), the evergreen sprouts new growth at the top of the tree. What makes this significant is that the new growth look exactly like little crosses. As I witnessed a group of trees sprouting new growth, it was a sight to behold. Several dozen crosses adorned the trees. It actually brought tears to my eyes.

Not long afterward I saw a TV piece on a galaxy that has a black hole—evidenced by an incredible cross shape.

I also learned that research has found that a human's DNA contains what is called "laminin," and it is undeniably cross shaped.

To me, all of these discoveries are not mere coincidences. They simply confirm the truth: God is in everything and He is alive!

December 2

He is a dream weaver,

A wave maker, a stirrer of the waters,

An awesome creator.

The windows of heaven

Are viewed through His eyes,

His limits are boundless,

His grace, undenied.

The babe in a manger,

That transformed the world,

Began when an angel

Came to visit a girl.

A world maker,

Heart changer.

Sin breaker.

An open door,

Of lives restored,

Cleansed and pure.

Be assured,

All this and more,

All things new,

Awaits when Christ abides in you.

December 3

If one only believes in the theory of cosmic happenstance, then miracles can be easily dismissed as nothing but quirks. Oh, but wonders of wonders, how the Word of God foretold: "I see him, but not now; I behold him, but not near; a star shall come forth from Jacob, a scepter shall rise from Israel, and shall crush through the forehead of Moab, and tear down all the sons of Sheth" (Numbers 24:17 NASB).

The miracle can be missed if you place logic in this equation. Miracles transcend logic. Don't spoil the extraordinary by mortal reasoning. It's way out of our realm of thinking. Just marvel at a brilliant star, which beckoned kings from across the world to seek His presence.

The universe will never be the same again, because the Messiah is here at last! And as we celebrate the miracle of His birth this month, remember He is still in the business of miracles. The true "spirit of Christmas" is in the belief of His magnificence—Jesus. Wise men still seek Him.

December 4

The season of giving is upon us. How wonderful and gratifying it is to give. But it does sometimes hurt when you do something great for someone and they do not appreciate it.

Not to worry! God is on the job. The Bible tells us that when we do something good, we should do it unto the Lord (Colossians 3:23). If no one seems to notice your good works, know that the Lord is watching everything. The Bible also says you shouldn't tell everyone to let them know about your good deeds (Matthew 6:1). The only One who has to know is God.

So why not do something this season to brighten someone's life? Be an "undercover" Santa: pay for the next person's order in the drive-thru, or give a toy to some charity like Toys for Tots. I promise you, it will warm your heart throughout the Christmas season. Fa-la-la-la-la!

But when you give to the needy, do not let your left hand know what your right hand is doing, so that your giving may be in secret. And your Father who sees in secret will reward you.

Matthew 6:3–4 (ESV)

December 5

With regard to many situations in the Bible, God had the chance to instantly change a dire circumstance. But He just let it ride. "Why would God put His beloved people in jeopardy?" you may ask.

Let us take for example David, who was anointed to be king of Israel after Saul, whom God had appointed to be ruler. But Saul soon began to neglect the voice of God's prophet.

Although David was "a man after [God's] own heart" (Acts 13:22 NIV), he endured numerous attempts on his life, because King Saul had grown jealous of him.

Twice David had the chance to kill Saul, but David said, "I will not touch God's anointed."
Why didn't God just step in and strike down Saul to rescue David?

Many times, when we are facing a battle of our own, we pray for God's intervention. Perhaps there is a lesson to be learned in all this.

With every battle David fought, God was helping him to build his faith for future battles.

Likewise, in every battle we fight, we can gain ground. Yes, it can feel quite the challenging task. But God is standing by and girding us with His strength, as we put our trust in Him.

His Word promises, "Behold, I give unto you power to tread on serpents and scorpions, and over all the power of the enemy: and nothing shall by any means hurt you" (Luke 10:19 KJV).

December 6

When a precious lady referred to me as an "angel," I answered, "No, I am far from an angel."

Later on when I told my witty daughter about this, she said, "Mom, you are like Clarence—the angel from *It's a Wonderful Life!*"

But the lady's compliment had me thinking: Aren't we all in a way a sort of "Clarence"? We struggle and strive to do good, but, like Clarence, in our own foolhardy way we fumble. Try as we might to earn our "wings" by working in our own strength, we can never obtain God's favor by works.

As Paul said in Ephesians 2:8–9 (NIV): "For it is by grace you have been saved, through faith—and this is not from yourselves, it is the gift of God— not by works, so that no one can boast."

But should we stop doing good works because we do not have to? Heavens no!

We do not *have* to do good works—we get to!

And the reward, my friends, in those deeds is a warm heart and the satisfaction of knowing we did something to help someone.

It truly is a wonderful life!

December 7

The woman said to me, "Why did you get me these things? When I saw the gift, I thought it was a mistake."

Later I received an email from her that said, *"I was in shock to receive such thoughtful gifts. You got me everything I love! You must really know me. I can't tell you how much I appreciate your thoughtfulness. You are a very special lady and I am so glad we work together."*

My reply: *"Did you ever read the book* When God Winks? *Consider this a God wink. He loves you very much. You are a very special lady. Have a blessed Christmas!"*

The warmth I felt in my heart at that moment could melt any ice Jack Frost could muster up.

Then I saw her near the stairwell on Christmas Eve. She said with a sweet smile, "Merry Christmas, special lady."

I smiled back and said, "Merry Christmas."

And I felt God smiling too.

Let us all live to make God smile.

December 8

From almost the time of His conception, Jesus faced opposition. In fact anyone associated with our Lord had to endure much persecution. Mary, Joseph, and Jesus's lives were in great danger as soon as He was born. Why would a new born baby pose such a threat to a powerful ruler? Could it be that even the unbelievers knew the power Jesus possessed?

The enemy of our souls is very much aware of our Lord, and he knows who belongs to Him. Is it any wonder Christians have been persecuted for centuries?

The battle is not personal, it is spiritual. But we can have the confidence that the baby in the manger was and is the one and only Savior who was nailed to the cross for our salvation.

That is why we have an enemy.

That is why we have victory.

Our victor is Jesus Christ.

December 9

Love came alive for me Christmas,

I realized I am never alone.

My Savior, His life gave the ransom,

To ensure our eternal home.

His birth, His sole reason for coming,

Is love at its greatest expense.

He gave all He had at that wood cross,

The eternal love letter sent.

He began in a lowly stable,

His life was at stake from the start.

A babe in a manger was able

Give a love to win over our hearts.

Now we are never alone here.

We may feel we are alone inside,

Jesus, His presence keeps giving,

The best Christmas gift for all time.

December 10

The brilliance of the star brought wise men from across the lands to worship the King whom the prophets foretold:

> *Therefore the Lord himself will give you a sign: The virgin will conceive and give birth to a son, and will call him Immanuel.* (Isaiah 7:14 NIV)

> *For to us a child is born, to us a son is given, and the government will be on his shoulders. And he will be called Wonderful Counselor, Mighty God, Everlasting Father, Prince of Peace.* (Isaiah 9:6 NIV)

> *But you, Bethlehem Ephrathah, though you are small among the clans of Judah, out of you will come for me one who will be ruler over Israel, whose origins are from of old, from ancient times.* (Micah 5:2 NIV)

There was a force, drawing many in toward Bethlehem and the baby. What was this force, beckoning men to gather in a lowly stable? The power of God came to earth that day in the form of a newborn child—a babe brought forth to take away the sins of this world, to take upon Himself all the hate, pain, and wrath of mankind.

If we will only take some time to absorb the enormity of it all. His presence is the most awesome present of all. He is the reason for the season.

December 11

All the bright lights and tinsel in the world gathered together cannot outshine the brilliance of Jesus. Think of it: God came down as a man, for the remission of all sin, to save us from eternal damnation.

His light is illumination for any dark corner in our minds and hearts.

His grace is sufficient to forgive and heal.

This tiny babe, born in a manger, is the sole Savior of the world.

The star of Bethlehem beckoned men to come honor and worship the true star of the universe, the bright and shining one—the Messiah!

I am ... the bright Morning Star.
Revelation 22:16 (NIV)

December 12

Love is a gift that never stops giving! We are approaching Christmas, the day of receiving and giving gifts. It's a season of perpetual hope. Yet, what if everyone continued the idea of giving all through the year? How delightful would that be?

I am not talking about presents and packages with bows. I am referring to the true meaning of the season: peace on earth, goodwill toward men.

A smile, or a heartfelt "How are you?" or "Have a beautiful day!" speaks volumes to someone who is hungry for hope. Let us begin by beginning today and carrying love with us wherever we go.

It begins with me; with you. We have the power to give presents with our very presence.

Pass it on. It could be contagious.

December 13

"Emotional and spiritual maturity is determined by how you treat those who do not treat you right." This powerful quote came from a teaching I heard recently.

I admit I am faced with a challenge when I am treated unkindly by another person. My first impulse is to get defensive to protect myself. But as we examine the Scriptures, we learn that this is not God's plan for us:

> *You have heard that it was said, "Love your neighbor and hate your enemy." But I tell you, love your enemies and pray for those who persecute you, that you may be children of your Father in heaven. He causes his sun to rise on the evil and the good, and sends rain on the righteous and the unrighteous. If you love those who love you, what reward will you get? And if you greet only your own people, what are you doing more than others? Be perfect, therefore, as your heavenly Father is perfect.*
> (Matthew 5:43–48)

In the world we are taught to stand up for ourselves. But in everything God wants us to convey an attitude of godliness so that others can see Him in us. As Christians, then, let us exude Godliness in both word and deed.

December 14

It was the Christmas of 2006. I was driving home after working a late shift and feeling pretty much alone in the world. I knew God was there for me; I knew God was real. But on this night I asked God for a real-time Christmas wish. I wanted and needed to see tangible proof that His love was there for me that evening.

Before the wished thought was even finished processing in my head, I looked up in the sky and saw the most brilliant star I'd ever seen. I do not claim it to be the "Christmas star" that pointed the way to the manger and baby Jesus. But it was my Christmas star, and it filled me with a sense of peace and a new hope for the future.

On that night of nights, love came down for me at Christmas.

December 15

Stand aside and let the mystery of God overtake you. You may not understand the whole picture, but just look at one piece of the puzzle. Whether that piece be a corner, or from the middle, build upon that.

It may take time. But that is all we have. Go on and give Him the floor. And know that you don't have to be a visionary to witness the happening. He's creating a new thing. So throw all your blueprints away.

And remember that you don't have to know where it's all going. Just trust! Quit trying to figure it all out. Just hand Him the remnants of your broken dreams and shattered heart. And do not feel like you have to grovel. He doesn't care if you've let Him down. He only cares why you do not trust Him to pull it all together.

Make this day count and say, "Here, God, take my life and do something with it."

You will never regret it. I promise.

December 16

Once a cold, dark winter's night,
A young girl wandered in the snow.
Alone, there was no soul in sight,
She felt frozen to the bone.
She searched to find a spot to rest,
Somewhere safe and warm,
Afraid and lost, she could only guess
Which direction she would turn.
Suddenly she heard a voice,
And in a soft and gentle tone,
It said to her, "The greater choice
Would be to take the higher road."
She obeyed and then began to walk,
At a turn, she saw a light,
It beckoned her with warmth and love,
She felt hopeful with its sight.
A candle in the window,
Brightly glowed through the winter's frost,
She knew at once, she was finally home,
No more, did she feel lost.
She felt the peace to try the door,
And she let herself right in,
There, the one who awaited her,
Her Savior and her friend.

December 17

Love came down at Christmas. And love stayed faithful all the way to the cross.

The Bible says, "Love never fails" (1 Corinthians 13:8 NKJV). But how many times have we failed love?

We gave up, threw in the towel, just up and quit! But Jesus remained faithful and true all the way through to the cross and the grave! It was tough for Him—real, real tough! He endured the pain and hate while wearing the flesh of a man. Yes, He was God. But He was God in the flesh. He hurt like us. He bled like us. Yet He was without sin. He was, is, and always will be phenomenal, awesome, sinless.

Yes, love came down at Christmas, and He never stops loving, ever!

December 18

Don't belabor the idea of just giving it over to Him. With Christmas approaching, many of us feel overwhelmed by the daunting task of getting it all done. Every year there is a mad rush for "stuff," often beginning in October—whether it's gifts to give or decorations to put up or treats to bake. What enormous pressure we put upon ourselves! No wonder, after all the time and expense, we feel disheartened after it is all over.

It is time to reclaim our peace! This year, let us make a point to ask God for His serenity throughout the Christmas season. No more attempts at micromanaging it all! Just breathe and say, "Jesus."

Give it all to Him. He will show you how to let go and bask in the glow of the knowledge. He is the reason for the season!

For to us a child is born, to us a son is given, and the government will be on his shoulders. And he will be called Wonderful Counselor, Mighty God, Everlasting Father, Prince of Peace. Of the greatness of his government and peace there will be no end. He will reign on David's throne and over his kingdom, establishing and upholding it with justice and righteousness from that time on and forever. The zeal of the LORD Almighty will accomplish this.
Isaiah 9:6–7 (NIV)

December 19

At this time of year, it is easy to forget the ones who are left behind. While we are out and about, shopping for our holiday feast, the so-called dregs of our society are among us, hidden in the shadows. Not a very cheerful thought, is it?

But the truth remains, whether we recognize it or not. The problems that plague our world can be resolved with one single act of kindness at a time.

Hiding from the truth never makes it less true. Given our capabilities, we have the potential to end poverty and hunger on a national scale. Wouldn't it be phenomenal if everyone in this country just started doing something now?

It wouldn't cost much for everyone to just do one thing. The dividends would pay off as we spread kindness far and wide.

We can make it possible. It all can start with me and you!

December 20

It's living for our God at all costs! Keep believing in a better world, no matter how it appears. Naysayers may kick sand in your face and scoff at you. But God is on your side and He won't let you down.

Keep professing that the glass is half full. You may be the minority. But when you lay your head down at night, you will be at peace. Though the angst of the world may come to nip at your heels, don't fret. God has your back. And He will be steadfast to help you fight for what is good, pure, and worthwhile.

As Paul said in 1 Timothy 6:12 (NLT): "Fight the good fight for the true faith. Hold tightly to the eternal life to which God has called you, which you have declared so well before many witnesses."

Though the opposition is real, God will give you the strength and abilities to stave off the power of the enemy: "Behold, I give unto you power to tread on serpents and scorpions, and over all the power of the enemy: and nothing shall by any means hurt you" (Luke 10:19 KJV).

Though the battle may not be physical, it is exhausting just the same. But He needs you now—for such a time as this. Be a foot soldier in God's army. He wants you!

December 21

It was a Saturday in December and it was pouring down
rain. I was driving through a neighboring town, and as I
started down a desolate stretch of road near a local steel
mill, I noticed three figures walking along in the torrential
downpour under a little, and mostly ineffective, umbrella: a
young man and two small boys.

As I drove past them, I knew what I had to do. My
car was filled with laundry and shopping bags. But I
stopped alongside the road in town, pushed everything out
of the way on my seat, and then drove back.

I approached and rolled down my window. "Would
you like a ride?" I asked.

"Yes, thank you," replied the young man.

The kids jumped in and they introduced themselves.
They told me with much excitement they were coming
from a free toy giveaway and they showed me their boxes
of Legos. The littlest boy said he was so happy to have his
toy and he couldn't wait to play.

I drove them a few miles, which wasn't far at all,
but it would seem plenty far if you were walking in pouring
rain, with two little ones who couldn't walk very fast.
We arrived at an old house that sat by itself on a long road.
As they got out, the young man thanked me and I wished
them a Merry Christmas. As they walked inside, I said a
little prayer right there and then, hoping they would have a
good Christmas with more than just toys.
But all the love they could hold in their hearts.

December 22

Do my prayers count? The answer is most definitely yes!

The enemy of our souls would like nothing more than for us to believe our prayers do not work. But the Bible states, "The effectual fervent prayer of a righteous man availeth much" (James 5:16 KJV). So do not worry if you don't feel worthy to receive answers for prayers. It is not our own merit, but Jesus's sacrifice that determines our worthiness.

Prayer is the direct conduit between us and God. It serves as a powerful weapon in transforming lives. But many feel their prayers are not heard and they succumb to hopelessness. Praying in agreement with another is a most effective tool to transforming any situation, no matter how dire it may be. As it says in Matthew 18:20 (KJV): "For where two or three are gathered together in my name, there am I in the midst of them." And there is exponentially more strength and power in numbers: "How should one chase a thousand, and two put ten thousand to flight, except their Rock had sold them, and the LORD had shut them up?" (Deuteronomy 32:30).

So I encourage you to continue to pray, no matter how hopeless it all looks. Even if it has been years, and the answer has not come to fruition, keep praying and believing.

The times when we fall apart are the times we've essentially given up hope. But remember this: no matter how hopeless we feel, God will never give up on us!

December 23

Oh Lord, You are glorious and magnificent,

All praise belongs to You. Almighty is the Lamb.

You are the same yesterday, today, and tomorrow,

And Your endless blessings carry no sorrow.

I bring all the wounds, the bruises of this life,

I lay them at Your feet, You heal me with Your sighs.

You challenge me to change myself,

 Transcending me to Your life-filled well.

I once was lost, but now I am found,

I was tattered and in pieces, I am covered by You now.

I bow down and remain humbled by Your sight,

I wait for Your guidance; in You, I will abide.

Like the deer who pants for water,

I will long for You evermore, my Father.

December 24

Somewhere buried beneath the heavy weight of humanity lies a grain of hope. No matter how small it may seem to you, even if it's the size of a pinhead, grab on to it and never let it go!

Though you feel that familiar sinking feeling of despair, keep looking up. No, it's not a picnic pressing on in the pain. But it's infinitely better than drowning in sorrow.

Do not focus on the present state of affairs. Forge on with the words, "I can do all things through Christ who strengthens me" resounding in your heart.

Things have been better, sure. But they've also been worse. Focus on how far you've come thus far.

You may think, *You don't know my problems. It'll take a miracle to fix this mess.* Lucky for you, God is in the miracle business! And you are more than lucky: you are blessed because Almighty God is in your corner and He will not let you fall between the cracks of life.

You may feel that you are down for the count. But this isn't your swan song.

The Lord is right there walking beside you.

So let us rejoice in advance, for we place our faith in the One who takes pleasure in our happiness.

The LORD be exalted, who delights in the well-being of his servant.
Psalm 35:27 (NIV)

December 25

Many come to honor Christ on this day. They believe in the deity, power, and love He possesses.

But countless others remain lost in a dying world. I see it every day and so does He.

He beckons them—the proud, the spiritually ignorant—to take a chance. Whether people, or life itself, have tried to decimate your heart and you now are afraid, know that He can be trusted. He is relentless in His pursuit of the lost.

Jesus came as an innocent babe in a lowly manger, so we need not be intimidated by His glory and kingship. As the angels spoke, "Fear not: for, behold, I bring you good tidings of great joy, which shall be to all people" (Luke 2:10 KJV).

He was born for those first ones to call on Him, just as He is here for the very last. The spotless Lamb who came to seek the hopeless. He will never, ever give up on you.

Jesus Christ believes in you. Do you believe in Him?

Merry Christmas!

December 26

Come to Jesus. But don't come alone. If we only see ourselves saved, what good is that?

Equate it to being on a large lifeboat. You see people in the water all around you, and they are in danger of drowning. You have the chance to save them. Some think they are good swimmers, and they do not desire your help. Then there are those who can barely keep their heads above water. They are desperately reaching out to be rescued. You know that if any of these do not all come aboard, they will surely perish.

Salvation is like that lifeboat. There are those who feel they do not need God. They think they are doing just fine. Then there are those who are desperately searching, and they are eager to get saved. Although both groups differ from each other, they both equally need God.

It does not matter that a person may think or feel that God doesn't exist. The fact is, He is God. Rather than arguing the point with a nonbeliever, pray for them. Your prayers may be the answer to save them from the worst possible demise: eternal separation from God.

And for those who are eager for salvation? Grab hold of their hand and pull them in. God will take care of the rest.

Without God we would all drown in sin and iniquity. Jesus is truly our lifesaver.

Then Jesus told them this parable: "Suppose one of you has a hundred sheep and loses one of them. Doesn't he leave the ninety-nine in the open country and go after the lost sheep until he finds it? And when he finds it, he joyfully puts it on his shoulders and goes home. Then he calls his friends and neighbors together and says, 'Rejoice with me; I have found my lost sheep.' I tell you that in the same way there will be more rejoicing in heaven over one sinner who repents than over ninety-nine righteous persons who do not need to repent.

Luke 15:3–7 (NIV)

December 27

This is dedicated to all the dear ones who have lost someone in recent times and are now missing them at Christmas time.

Your thank-you cards to family and friends have long since been mailed. The well-wishers have little by little disappeared, and the phone hardly rings at all.

But your tears still flow. Your heart has settled into a dull ache.

Now the Christmas tree and carols on the radio remind you of them. Everything stirs bittersweet nuances of the many Christmases spent together.

If this is you, may you call out to the One who loves and comforts you: "God, do you know how I feel inside? Can Christmas ever be wonderful again? I pray, Lord, that I can breathe in the peace that surrounds this season of hope. Help me to once again feel the love of Christmas while remembering the gift of love filled memories of Christmases past."

December 28

I prayed the prayer of faith with an elderly person yesterday. The person had been very ill, and wanted assurance of their salvation. Even though this precious senior could not put two sentences together, they repeated the prayer verbatim.

God does not care if an individual has the presence of mind to comprehend the prayer. He is merely concerned with one's intention.

The words this person spoke to me sounded so sad, because they believed God may not want to forgive them of their sins. I assured the person that God is eager to forgive, even though we are fearful He won't.

Together we listened to and sang a few traditional church hymns, and then I read some inspirational words to help them feel peace.

At the end of the conversation, I announced, "Well, we just had church!"

The person smiled. "Yes! Yes, we did!"

I believe that the prayer of this individual reached the throne room of God. The very moment they prayed, their life was totally transformed.

December 29

If we were to name one way to overcome hindrances and pray effectively, it would be to love. As Paul said in Galatians 5:14 (AMPCE): "For the whole Law ... is complied with in the one precept, You shall love your neighbor as [you do] yourself."

In studying the Bible, you will find more scriptures commanding us to love than any other commandment in the Bible. In John 13:34 (AMPCE), Jesus commanded us to love: "I give you a new commandment: that you should love one another. Just as I have loved you, so you too should love one another."

First Corinthians 13:1 (NIV) states: "If I speak in the tongues of men or of angels, but do not have love, I am only a resounding gong or a clanging cymbal." The entire thirteenth chapter of 1 Corinthians is devoted to defining what love is and what it is not. In verse 8, it spells it out simply by saying, "Love never fails" (NIV). In essence what God requires of us (in order to not have our prayers hindered), is to love unconditionally (*agape* love). By walking in God's love (not a humanistic view of what we think love is), we can overcome any sin, any obstacle, no matter how large it may seem.

First Peter 4:8 (AMPCE) says, "Above all things have intense and unfailing love for one another, for love covers a multitude of sins...." Remember, love is only a word until we put it into action.

December 30

Although the season of winter enfolds me,

I will claim it is spring within,

I refuse to stand by, just surrender,

I will not let the coldness come in.

The snow, in its fury, is blowing,

The icicles are waiting at bay,

But the warmth from God's Spirit engulfs me,

In His presence, I know I am safe.

The wind and the cold, how they mock me,

They scoff, I am blind to their sight,

Still, out of the depths of this heart springs,

A great garden, His own Spirit's delight.

Isaiah 35:2 It shall blossom abundantly and rejoice even with joy and singing.

December 31

Did you know you are an original work of art? Isn't it wonderful how God designed us all to be a one-of-a-kind? There is no mistake: God intended it to be that way. God is into details. It is said that if we examined all the snow that has fallen, we would find no two snowflakes are alike. Although He has created us to be diverse, we are to share one commonality: Christ. For we were all molded in His image as believers (Romans 8:29).

"For we [no matter how] numerous we are, are one body, because we all partake of the one Bread… (1 Corinthians 10:17 AMPCE). Being one with Christ means putting our flesh under to serve our brothers and sisters. When someone is hurting, we should be there—not on our behalf, but in Christ's stead.

We are to be living examples of Christ so that He, not us, may be exalted.

If we are not in union with one another as a body (God's church), this is not possible. If there is strife, bitterness, envy, or resentment in the body, we cannot function at the capacity God wills for us to serve Him. At His coming, Jesus expects to find a church "without spot or blemish and at peace" (2 Peter 3:14 AMPCE).

Remember, if we are to be one with Christ, we are to be united as one body.

Consider what the apostle Paul said: "For just as the body is a unity and yet has many parts, and all the parts though many, form [only] one body, so it is with Christ ..." (1 Corinthians 12:12 AMPCE). And also think about what was said of the early church: "And all who believed ... were united and [together] they had everything in common.... And day after day they regularly assembled in the temple with united purpose ..." (Acts 2:44, 46 AMPCE).

As the Word clearly conveys, we must continually be in a state of "oneness" if we are to live as one body. Once united in His will, then we may be called the true body of Christ, His church. We should remain consistent, striving to obtain this unity by daily yielding to the voice of our Lord, and residing (living) in His Word.

Made in the USA
Middletown, DE
05 April 2024

52469490R00215